CAN'T WON'T COOK COOK
2

KEVIN WOODFORD

Photos by Juliet Piddington

BBC BOOKS

This book is published to accompany the television series *Can't Cook Won't Cook*
which is produced by Bazal Midlands for BBC Birmingham
Executive Producer: Linda Clifford
Producer: Caroline Officer

Published by BBC Books,
an imprint of BBC Worldwide Ltd,
Woodlands, 80 Wood Lane, London W12 0TT

First published in 1997
Compiled by Bazal Productions
Recipes by Orla Broderick and Susie Magasiner,
copyright © Kevin Woodford 1997
Photographs by Juliet Piddington,
copyright © BBC Worldwide Ltd 1997

ISBN 0 563 38361 5

Recipes edited by Susanna Tee
Home economy by Sarah Ramsbottom
Set in Gill Sans, News Gothic, Poppl-Laudatio and 55 Helvetica Roman
Printed in Great Britain by Martins the Printers Ltd, Berwick-upon-Tweed
Bound in Great Britain by Hunter & Foulis Ltd, Edinburgh
Colour separation by DOT Gradations Limited, Wickford, Essex
Cover printed by Belmont Press Limited, Northampton

Contents

Introduction

Hello, let me welcome you to *Can't Cook Won't Cook* Book 2 which, like the TV series, aims to help you rise to the challenge of cookery. Indeed, by following my recipes you will be able to tickle the taste buds of your friends and family with adventurous dishes which are simple to make and fun to prepare. (After all, I only have 30 minutes on the show and look how many delightful dishes are produced!)

One of the reasons for the success of the TV series is that it demonstrates that even the most reluctant and inexperienced cooks can laugh their way through 30 minutes of lightning cookery, whilst at the same time preparing gourmet dishes that everyone can enjoy. Yes – cooking can be easy, especially if you follow my three golden rules for success: concentration, organization and presentation.

Concentration is an important ingredient for successful cookery, but oh, I hear you shout, what about the children, grandma or taking the dog for a walk! The secret is to pick a time to try out new recipes when you are least likely to be distracted. Then put on your favourite music, pop on your apron and enter the world of cooking for pleasure.

Organization is the main key to success. In a professional kitchen, young chefs are taught the art of *mise en place* – which simply means 'having everything to hand and ready'. So make sure you allow time for preparing your *mise en place* by reading the recipe carefully before you start to cook, setting out all the ingredients, arranging them close to your cooker in order of use and having any equipment you may need close to hand. By approaching cooking in such a methodical way, you are less likely to go wrong or miss out any ingredient.

For me, presentation is crucial – it allows the creative side of your nature to be expressed. The book includes lots of ideas on how to garnish the dishes but to ensure perfection always remember to:

- set the scene – any meal can be an occasion, so lay the table in advance
- warm (or chill) your serving plates before use depending upon whether the dish is hot or cold
- check that the food is seasoned correctly by tasting it before you serve
- have your garnishes ready!

Every time you produce a beautiful dish your confidence will grow and these recipes really are guaranteed to succeed. Now it's over to you, to rattle your pots and pans in order to tickle the taste buds of your nearest and dearest. Oh, and do be sure to have a gaggle of giggles whilst you're cooking!

Much love,

Before You Start

Read the recipe carefully before you start to make a dish so that you understand it totally. Then collect together the cooking equipment and all the ingredients you will need. Finally, weigh and measure out the ingredients. If you are a new cook, follow the recipe precisely to begin with, using the exact quantities and ingredients. When it comes to seasonings, herbs, flavourings, spices and sweetenings, however, they can usually be varied to suit individual tastes.

Basic Cooking Techniques

This alphabetical list is for you to refer to when you need a more detailed explanation of what to do when following a recipe.

BEAT To agitate an ingredient or mixture, using a wooden spoon, fork or whisk, to incorporate air and to make it smooth.

BLANCH To immerse food briefly in boiling water to remove skin, whiten it or destroy enzymes and preserve colour, flavour and texture, ready for freezing.

BLEND To mix foods together evenly using a spoon, food processor or electric blender.

BOIL To cook in a liquid, such as water, stock or milk, at a minimum temperature of 100°C/212°F, when the surface of the liquid will continuously show bubbles.

CARAMELISE To slowly heat sugar until it turns to liquid and goes brown.

CHOP To cut food into small pieces with a sharp knife.

COAT To cover food with a protective coating, such as batter, breadcrumbs or flour, before frying or covering food with a sauce.

CORE To remove the hard, indigestible centre of some foods, such as peppers, kidneys, apples, pears, pineapples.

CREAM To beat together fat and sugar until the mixture is pale and fluffy and resembles whipped cream.

CRUSH To break down food into smaller particles.

DICE To cut food into small, even-sized, cube-shaped pieces.

DISSOLVE To mix a dry or solid ingredient, applying heat if necessary, with a liquid until the mixture is clear.

DRAIN To remove any liquid or fat from foods by using a sieve, colander or draining spoon, or by placing food on absorbent kitchen paper.

DRY-FRY To fry without the use of extra fat or oil.

DUST To sprinkle food lightly with flour, sugar or other dry ingredient.

FLAKE To separate cooking fish into small pieces using two forks.

FLAMBÉ To ignite and burn a liqueur, which has been poured over food, to add the flavour of the alcohol.

FOLD To mix, using a large metal spoon to cut through and then gently lift up, a whisked or whipped food with other ingredients so that it retains its lightness.

FRY To cook food in hot fat or oil, either by immersing it completely or cooking in a little fat and turning the food.

GLAZE To give a glossy surface to a sweet or savoury dish.

GRATE To shave food into small shreds using a grater.

HULL To remove the calyx and stem from soft fruit.

KNEAD To combine ingredients, by hand, which are too stiff to stir.

LINE To add a protective covering to the base and/or sides of a cooking tin or dish.

MASH To beat or crush a soft mixture free from lumps, using a potato masher or fork.

MIX To combine two or more ingredients, using your hands, a spoon, fork, knife, electric mixer or food processor, depending on the ingredients.

PARE To thinly peel fruit or vegetables.

PEEL To remove the outer rind or shell from a food.

POACH To cook food in a liquid at a temperature of not more than 96°C/205°F so that the surface is just trembling.

ROLL OUT To flatten pastry or dough, using a rolling pin.

RUB IN To incorporate fat into flour until the mixture resembles fine breadcrumbs.

SAUTÉ To lightly fry in a little butter and/or oil.

SCRAPE To remove the outer layer of food.

SEAL To fry meat or poultry in hot fat to give colour and add flavour, and to encase a filling in pastry or other casing.

SEGMENT To remove the skin of citrus fruits and divide the flesh into natural portions.

SEPARATE To divide or separate one thing from another. Often used with reference to separating egg whites from yolks.

SHRED To finely cut food using a sharp knife.

SIFT To shake a dry ingredient, such as flour, through a sieve to remove any lumps.

SIMMER To cook food in a liquid kept just below boiling point.

SKIN To remove the outer coat or skin of a food.

SLICE To cut food into thin rounds or slices, using a sharp knife or food processor.

STIR To mix food gently in a circular movement, usually with a spoon.

STIR-FRY To cook thinly sliced foods quickly in a little very hot oil, in a wok or large frying pan, and stirring constantly.

STRAIN To pass a liquid through a sieve, colander or muslin cloth to remove any solids.

SWEAT To cook cut-up vegetables in a little fat over a gentle heat, covered, to dry out their juices.

TOSS To turn or flip food over lightly to coat with flour, seasoning or dressing.

TURN OUT To remove food from a tin in which it was cooked or a mould in which it was set. The turned-out food should retain its shape.

WHIP To beat a food or mixture, using a fork, balloon whisk, rotary whisk or electric whisk, until it is light and fluffy due to the incorporation of air.

WHISK To introduce air into egg whites, using a balloon whisk, rotary whisk or electric whisk, to increase their volume. Whisked egg whites should hold their shape.

ZEST To remove the coloured part of the rind of citrus fruits.

About the Recipes

Metric and imperial quantities are given in the recipes but never mix together as they are not interchangeable.

Sets of measuring spoons are available in both metric and imperial sizes to give accurate measurements of small quantities.

Spoon measures are level, unless otherwise stated.

Medium eggs are used in the recipes unless otherwise specified.

Granulated sugar is used in the recipes unless otherwise specified.

Basic Cooking Equipment

Having the right tool for the job really does make cooking easier and more pleasurable. Use this list as a guide to suit your needs.

General

chopping board
kitchen scales
measuring jug
measuring spoons
kettle
food processor
colander
rolling pin
mixing bowl
pudding basins
sieve
grater
set of pastry cutters
12.5 cm (5 in) ring moulds

Pots and Pans

very large saucepan
2 or 3 large pans with lids
non-stick milk pan
large frying pan or wok
    with a lid
non-stick omelette and
    pancake pan
ridged griddle pan
smooth griddle pan or
    heavy-based frying pan

Baking Dishes and Tins

2 round or oval ovenproof
    casserole dishes
flameproof dish
gratin dish
pie dish
baking tray
Swiss roll tin
bun tray
roasting tin
20 cm (8 in) flan ring
    or tin
2 sandwich tins
wire cooling rack
9 cm (3½ in) tartlet tins
ramekin dishes
23 cm (9 in) cake tin

Cutlery and Tools

wooden spoons
20 cm (8 in) long sharp
    knife
12 cm (5 in) vegetable or
    paring knife
bread knife
vegetable peeler with a
    swivel blade
forks
knives
tablespoons
teaspoons
slotted spoon
fish slice
spatula
cooking tongs
ladle
potato masher
wooden skewers
apple corer
apple wedger
can opener
corkscrew
balloon whisk or an
    electric whisk
kitchen scissors
pastry brush
melon baller
zester

MEAT
DISHES

Indian Spicy Lamb Cutlets *11*

Mediterranean Lamb and Vegetable Platter *12*

Chilli con Carne with Potato Wedges *13*

Kofta Kebabs with Houmous Sauce and Couscous Salad *14*

Stuffed Fillet of Lamb with New Potatoes and Almond Beans *15*

Roasted Lamb with Bulgar Wheat and Fiery Tomato Sauce *16*

Scalloped Shepherd's Pie *18*

Mexican Chilli with Spicy Rice *19*

Tagliatelle Bolognese *20*

Madeira Steak with Rosti *21*

Steak au Poivre *22*

Spicy Beef with Thai Jasmine Rice and Crispy Noodles *23*

Creamy Dijon Beef with Bubble and Squeak *24*

Sweet and Sour Pork *25*

Big Soup with Pesto Grills *26*

Toad-in-the-Holes with Onion Gravy and Vichy Carrots *27*

Bacon and Colcannon with Cider Sauce *28*

Roast Pork with Apple Sauté *29*

Pork and Noodle Soup with Sesame Prawn Toasts *30*

Cheesy Macaroni, Ham and Veggie Bake *31*

Pork Goulash *32*

Spring Stew with Pork, Orange and Beetroot *33*

Indian Spicy Lamb Cutlets

SERVES 2

A ridged griddle pan allows meat to cook without sitting in its own fat. So much healthier, and it gives the food a lovely finish.

2 large garlic cloves
½ teaspoon chilli powder
½ teaspoon fresh ginger purée
1 tablespoon tomato purée
4 lamb cutlets, trimmed
50g (2oz) sachet coconut cream
225g (8oz) basmati rice, well rinsed
1 cinnamon stick
2 cardamom pods
2 tablespoons sunflower oil, plus extra for brushing
1 large onion
2 teaspoons hot Madras curry powder
400g (14oz) can chopped tomatoes
2 teaspoons light muscovado sugar
2 teaspoons white wine vinegar
100g (4oz) button mushrooms
175g (6oz) fresh young spinach leaves
1½ teaspoons ground coriander
1 teaspoon garam masala
salt and freshly ground black pepper

❶ Crush the garlic and mix half with the chilli powder, ginger and 1 teaspoon of the tomato purée. Season generously with salt and pepper and rub into the cutlets. Set aside to marinate.

❷ Pour 600ml (1 pint) boiling water on to the coconut cream and stir until dissolved. Put the rice in a saucepan and pour in the coconut mixture. Break the cinnamon stick and add half. Crush the cardamom pods with the back of a knife. Add to the pan, bring to the boil, cover and cook for 10–12 minutes until the liquid has been absorbed.

❸ Heat the oil in a wok or frying pan. Thinly slice the onion, add to the wok and cook over a high heat until crispy and lightly golden.

❹ Pre-heat a ridged griddle pan. Brush it with a little oil and cook the lamb cutlets over a medium heat for about 10 minutes or until tender.

❺ Meanwhile, tip half of the onion into a small pan and stir in the curry powder. Pour in the tomatoes and add the remaining piece of cinnamon, the remaining 2 teaspoons of tomato purée, the sugar and vinegar. Season generously and simmer gently for 3–4 minutes until thickened and pulpy.

❻ Slice the mushrooms. Wash the spinach and remove the stalks. Add the remaining garlic to the wok and cook for 30 seconds. Add the coriander and garam masala and cook for 1 minute, stirring. Add the mushrooms and stir-fry for about 1 minute, then add the spinach, with only the water clinging to the leaves after washing, and cook for a few minutes until wilted. Season with salt and pepper.

❼ Arrange the lamb chops on warmed serving plates and add some rice and spinach. Serve with the tomato chutney.

Mediterranean Lamb and Vegetable Platter

SERVES 2

Your butcher will be happy to remove the bones and tie the cutlets into small rosettes for you, if you don't feel confident about doing this yourself.

4 tablespoons olive oil, plus extra for cooking
1 small aubergine
1 large courgette
4 open-cap mushrooms
1 small yellow pepper
1 bird's eye chilli (see below)
1 small shallot
1 garlic clove
1 tablespoon sun-dried tomato purée
1 tablespoon red wine vinegar
selection of chopped fresh herbs, to include oregano, parsley and marjoram
4 lamb cutlets
salt and freshly ground black pepper

1 Heat a large griddle or frying pan and brush with a little oil.

2 Cut the aubergine and courgette into 5mm (¼ in) slices. Quarter or halve the mushrooms if large. Cut the pepper in half, remove the core and seeds and then cut the flesh into eighths. Add to the pan with the mushrooms, aubergine and courgette. Drizzle over a little more oil and cook for 6–8 minutes, turning regularly.

3 Meanwhile, halve the chilli, scoop out the seeds and finely chop the flesh. Chop the shallot and crush the garlic. Put the chilli, shallot and garlic in a bowl with 4 tablespoons of the oil, the tomato purée, vinegar and some of the herbs. Season the dressing with salt and pepper.

4 Bone and roll the lamb cutlets and secure each with a piece of string. Spread 1 tablespoon of the dressing over each noisette.

5 Remove the vegetables from the pan, transfer to a shallow dish and keep warm. Add the lamb noisettes to the pan and cook for 3–4 minutes on each side.

6 While they are still hot, pour the remaining dressing over the vegetables and toss to coat.

7 Arrange the vegetables in the middle of warmed serving plates. Top with the lamb noisettes, sprinkle over a little more of the chopped herbs and serve at once.

Bird's eye chillies *are very tiny red chillies, the smallest you can find, with a slightly shrivelled skin. They have a very powerful hot flavour.*

Chilli con Carne with Potato Wedges

SERVES 2

If soured cream is difficult to obtain, you can make your own by mixing 1 teaspoon lemon juice into 150 ml (¼ pint) fresh double cream and leaving to stand for 30 minutes.

1 onion
1 tablespoon sunflower oil
250g (9oz) minced lamb
3 garlic cloves
1 teaspoon chilli powder
1 teaspoon ground cumin
400g (14oz) can chopped tomatoes
2 tablespoons tomato purée
1 large potato, baked and left until cold
2 tablespoons olive oil
a pinch of dried thyme
400g (14oz) can red kidney beans, rinsed and drained
2 rashers of rindless smoked streaky bacon
a small bunch of fresh chives
150ml (¼ pint) soured cream
1 spring onion
25g (1oz) Cheddar cheese
salt and freshly ground black pepper

❶ Pre-heat the grill.

❷ Finely chop the onion. Heat the sunflower oil in a large saucepan, add the onion and fry briefly before adding the mince. Cook until the meat is browned.

❸ Meanwhile, chop 2 garlic cloves and add to the meat with the chilli and cumin. Cook for 1 minute.

❹ Stir in the tomatoes, tomato purée and about 150ml (¼ pint) of water to make a sauce. Season well with salt and pepper to taste and leave to simmer.

❺ Cut the baked potato lengthways into 4 wedges. Cut out the potato, leaving a 1cm (½ in) strip inside the skin. Reserve the flesh and cut each wedge in half again. Place the wedges on a baking tray. Crush the remaining garlic clove into a purée with a little salt and mix with half the olive oil and the thyme. Brush the garlic oil over the potato wedges and grill for about 6 minutes until golden and hot.

❻ Roughly chop the reserved potato and add to the meat with the kidney beans, stirring to combine.

❼ Heat the remaining olive oil in a frying pan. Cut the bacon into strips, add to the pan and fry until golden.

❽ Finely chop the chives, reserving 6, and stir into the soured cream.

❾ Trim and cut the spring onion into diagonal slices. Remove the wedges from the grill and grate the cheese on top. Sprinkle over the spring onions and bacon and return to the grill. Cook for a further

1–2 minutes or until bubbling and golden.
10 Ladle the chilli into 2 serving bowls, standing on a serving plate. Season the potato wedges with plenty of pepper and arrange like petals around the chilli. Spoon a large dollop of the soured cream into the chilli. Arrange 3 chives over the top of each bowl and serve at once with the remaining soured cream as a dip for the potato wedges.

Kofta Kebabs with Houmous Sauce and Couscous Salad

SERVES 2

Couscous is tiny balls of semolina which are moistened with a liquid, usually stock. It is ready to be eaten when the liquid has been absorbed.

8fl oz (225ml) hot vegetable stock
juice of ½ a lemon
100g (4oz) pre-cooked couscous
1 garlic clove
225g (8oz) minced lamb
1 teaspoon ground cumin
¼ teaspoon cayenne
¼ teaspoon ground coriander
1 tablespoon olive oil, plus extra for cooking and serving
1 small fennel head
1 small courgette
2 spring onions
1 small red pepper
2 tablespoons houmous
2 tablespoons natural yogurt
4 large mint leaves
1 tablespoon chopped fresh coriander leaves
salt and freshly ground black pepper
lemon wedges and a little paprika, to garnish

1 Pour the stock and lemon juice over the couscous, stir and leave to swell.

2 Meanwhile, chop the garlic and mix together with the minced lamb, cumin, cayenne and ground coriander. Season with salt and pepper.

3 Soak four 15cm (6in) wooden skewers in warm water. Pre-heat a griddle or frying pan.

4 Roll the meat mixture into 4 sausage shapes. Insert the skewers down the length of the sausages and squeeze around the skewers. Heat a little of the oil on the griddle pan, add the kebabs and cook for about 10 minutes, until browned, turning occasionally.

5 Meanwhile, cut the fennel into small pieces. Quarter the courgette lengthways and cut into small dice. Cut the spring onions into 1cm (½in) lengths. Cut the pepper into quarters then finely dice the flesh, discarding the core and seeds.

6 Heat a second frying pan and add 1 tablespoon of the olive oil. Add the fennel, courgette, spring onions and pepper to the pan and stir-fry over a high heat for a few minutes to char slightly.

7 To make the sauce, mix together the houmous and yogurt. Chop the mint leaves and add, with salt and pepper if necessary.

8 Mix the vegetables into the couscous. To serve, spoon the couscous salad on to warmed serving plates and sprinkle the coriander on top. Arrange the kebabs on top and spoon over some of the houmous sauce. Drizzle over some olive oil and sprinkle with paprika. Garnish with a wedge of lemon.

....

Houmous *is a Middle Eastern dip made from a purée of cooked chick peas, olive oil, tahini (sesame seed paste), lemon juice and garlic. It is sold in tubs and you will find it in the chilled cabinets of most supermarkets.*

....

Stuffed Fillet of Lamb with New Potatoes and Almond Beans

SERVES 2

....

An ordinary piece of meat is transformed into a delicious dish. Clever cooking doesn't mean hard work, just a few moments of your time!

200g (7oz) baby new potatoes
1 small onion
1 small garlic clove
2 tablespoons olive oil
2 teaspoons chopped fresh rosemary
1 small lemon
25g (1oz) white breadcrumbs
4 ready-to-eat dried apricots
1 lamb fillet, weighing about 225g (8oz)
50ml (2fl oz) red wine
100g (4oz) mange-tout peas
25g (1oz) butter
120ml (4fl oz) lamb stock
1 teaspoon redcurrant jelly
15g (½oz) flaked almonds
salt and freshly ground black pepper
sprigs of rosemary, to garnish

1 Pre-heat the oven to 200°C/400°F/Gas 6.

2 Put the potatoes in a covered saucepan of cold salted water, bring to the boil and simmer for 15–20 minutes until tender.

3 Meanwhile, finely chop the onion and garlic. Heat 1 tablespoon of the olive oil in a frying pan. Add the onion, garlic and half of the chopped rosemary. Grate in half of the lemon rind. Remove from the heat and mix with the breadcrumbs. Season with salt and pepper. Quarter the apricots and add to the mixture.

4 Make a slit down the length of the lamb and gently open out the fillet. Do not cut all the way through. Press the bread stuffing into the fillet. Reshape the fillet and tie together with string, 6 times.

5 Heat the remaining tablespoon of oil in the pan you made the stuffing in, add the lamb and brown on all sides to seal. Transfer to a small baking dish and roast in the oven for 8–10 minutes until tender, turning occasionally.

6 Pour the wine into the pan. Add the remaining rosemary and boil rapidly to reduce by half.

7 Meanwhile, slice the mange-tout diagonally in half. Drain the potatoes and return to the pan with half the butter. Season with salt and pepper.

8 Add the lamb stock to the reduced wine and whisk in the redcurrant jelly and season with pepper. Simmer, whisking in a little of the butter just before you are ready to serve.

9 Melt the rest of the butter in a frying pan. Add the flaked almonds and cook until golden. Add the mange-tout and a good squeeze of lemon juice and stir-fry for 2–3 minutes until tender.

10 Lift the lamb on to a plate. Remove the string and cut the fillet into 6 thick slices. Arrange 3 slices on each warmed serving plate and spoon some of the sauce around the lamb. Arrange the mange-tout and potatoes on the plate. Garnish with rosemary sprigs and serve at once.

Roasted Lamb with Bulgar Wheat and Fiery Tomato Sauce

SERVES 2

Bulgar wheat is cracked or kibbled wheat of Middle Eastern origin. It requires very little cooking and makes a really interesting accompaniment to lamb.

1 red onion	**FOR THE FIERY TOMATO SAUCE**
½ yellow pepper	1 onion
100g (4oz) bulgar wheat	2 garlic cloves
300ml (½ pint) hot vegetable stock	2.5cm (1in) piece of fresh root ginger
grated rind and juice of 1 lemon	4 red chillies
about 3 tablespoons olive oil	2 tablespoons olive oil
1 lamb fillet, weighing about 225g (8oz)	400g (14oz) can plum tomatoes
1 garlic clove	a pinch of sugar
1 tablespoon snipped fresh chives, plus extra to garnish	
3 tablespoons chopped fresh parsley	
salt and freshly ground black pepper	

1 Finely chop the onion. Remove the core and seeds from the pepper and finely dice the flesh. Place the bulgar wheat in a large

16

bowl and pour over the stock, lemon juice, and 2 tablespoons of olive oil. Stir in the chopped onion and pepper and set aside for 20 minutes, stirring occasionally, until the grains have swollen and absorbed the liquid.

2 Pre-heat the oven to 220°C/425°F/Gas 7.

3 Make a slit down the length of the lamb and gently open out the fillet. Finely chop the garlic. Brush the lamb with a little olive oil and sprinkle over the chopped garlic, lemon rind, chives and half the chopped parsley. Season well with salt and pepper. Fold the fillet in half again and secure with cocktail sticks.

4 Place in a roasting tin and brush with a little olive oil. Sprinkle over salt and pepper then roast in the oven for 12 minutes until well browned but still pink in the centre.

5 Meanwhile, make the tomato sauce: Roughly chop the onion, garlic and ginger. Cut the chillies in half, remove the seeds and finely chop the flesh. Heat the olive oil in a saucepan, add the onion, garlic, ginger and chillies and fry for 3–4 minutes until softened. Add the tomatoes, sugar and plenty of salt and pepper. Bring to the boil, cover and simmer for 5 minutes.

6 Season the soaked bulgar wheat and stir in the remaining chopped parsley.

7 Remove the lamb from the oven and leave to rest for 2 minutes.

8 Using a hand blender or food processor, purée the tomato sauce.

9 Spoon the bulgar wheat on to warmed serving plates. Slice the lamb and arrange on top of the bulgar wheat and garnish with chives. Pour the tomato sauce around the lamb and serve at once.

••

Stock *For convenience, use a stock cube when a recipe calls for stock but, when it comes to seasoning the dish, go easy on the salt as most brands are very salty.*

Scalloped Shepherd's Pie

SERVES 2

The vegetables that accompany this dish are glazed with cider, mustard and honey and not only do they taste divine, they also look fabulous.

1 small onion
2 tablespoons sunflower oil
50g (2oz) button mushrooms
350g (12oz) lean minced lamb
1 bay leaf
1 large baking potato
175g (6oz) swede
1 large carrot
450ml (¾ pint) chicken stock
1 tablespoon plain flour
1 tablespoon tomato purée
1 tablespoon Worcestershire sauce
1 teaspoon Dijon mustard
2 tablespoons dry cider
1 teaspoon sugar
40g (1½oz) Cheddar cheese
1 tablespoon chopped fresh parsley
salt and freshly ground black pepper

1 Pre-heat the grill.

2 Finely chop the onion. Heat the oil in a sauté or frying pan. Add the onion and cook until softened.

3 Meanwhile, slice the mushrooms and add to the pan, stirring until well combined.

4 Add the lamb and bay leaf to the pan and cook for a further 2–3 minutes until browned, stirring to break up any lumps.

Season with salt and pepper.

5 Peel and slice the potato and put in a pan of boiling salted water. Cook for about 5 minutes until just tender, then drain and leave to cool.

6 Meanwhile, peel and cut the swede into thick slices. Peel the carrot, cut in half, then cut into thick slices. Put the swede and carrot in a saucepan with 300ml (½ pint) of the stock. Simmer for about 5 minutes until just tender.

7 Add the flour to the lamb and cook for 1 minute, stirring. Then add the tomato purée, Worcestershire sauce and the remaining stock, cover and simmer gently for 6–8 minutes until tender.

8 Blend the mustard with the cider and sugar. Drain the vegetables and add the cider mixture to the pan. Cook over a high heat until the liquid is syrupy.

9 Place the lamb in a flameproof dish (13 x 22cm/5 x 8½ in or thereabouts), remove the bay leaf and arrange the potatoes on top. Grate the cheese over the top and grill until golden.

10 Season the vegetables with salt and pepper and stir in the parsley. Serve with the pie.

Mexican Chilli with Spicy Rice

SERVES 2–3

With a little experience you will soon learn to adjust recipes like this one, by increasing or decreasing ingredients to suit your taste.

225g (8oz) long-grain rice
4 tablespoons sunflower oil
1 large red onion
1 large garlic clove
225g (8oz) lean minced beef
100g (4oz) button mushrooms
½ teaspoon ground cumin
a large pinch of hot chilli powder
225g (8oz) jar tomato and chilli taco sauce
200g (7oz) can chopped tomatoes
200g (7oz) can black-eye or kidney beans, rinsed and drained
1 lime
1 large red chilli
1 small courgette
50g (2oz) frozen sweetcorn kernels
a small bunch of fresh coriander
about 4 tablespoons soured cream
salt and freshly ground black pepper

Chillies *When preparing chillies, treat with care as their volatile oil can make your skin tingle. Wash your hands thoroughly afterwards and avoid rubbing your eyes*

1 Put the rice in a saucepan with plenty of boiling salted water and cook for about 10 minutes until nearly tender.

2 Heat half the oil in a sauté or frying pan. Chop the onion and add two-thirds to the pan, stirring to coat. Cook for 2–3 minutes.

3 Crush the garlic and add to the pan. Cook, stirring, for another 30 seconds. Add the beef and cook until browned, stirring occasionally. Slice the mushrooms, add to the pan and cook for a further 1–2 minutes.

4 Add the cumin and a little of the chilli powder, if liked, and cook for about 30 seconds. Add the taco sauce, tomatoes and beans and bring to the boil.

5 Squeeze the juice out of the lime and stir into the pan. Reduce the heat and simmer gently for 8–10 minutes, stirring occasionally.

6 Cut the red chilli in half and finely slice the flesh, discarding the seeds. Heat the rest of the oil in another frying pan and add the remaining onion. Cook for 1–2 minutes stirring. Add the sliced chilli, stirring to coat, and continue to cook over a low heat for 1–2 minutes. Add a sprinkling of the chilli powder to taste.

7 Drain the rice and rinse well under cold running water.

8 Dice the courgette and add to the sliced chilli. Add the rice and sweetcorn. Stir-fry for 2–3 minutes until the rice is tender and the vegetables are tender. Season with salt and pepper to taste.

⑨ Spoon the rice into a small, oiled ring mould and turn out on to warmed serving plates. Roughly chop the coriander. Spoon the chilli into the middle of the rice, add a swirl of soured cream and sprinkle the coriander on top. Serve at once.

Tagliatelle Bolognese
SERVES 4

If you are not a beef-eater, simply substitute minced lean lamb for the beef and follow the recipe exactly.

½ a celery stick
2 shallots
3 rashers of smoked streaky bacon
1 large garlic clove
2 tablespoons olive oil
400g (14oz) lean minced beef
120ml (4fl oz) red wine
400g (14oz) can chopped tomatoes
1 tablespoon tomato purée
1 teaspoon balsamic vinegar
a few drops of Worcestershire sauce
½ teaspoon caster sugar
a few drops of Tabasco sauce
175ml (6fl oz) beef stock
1 bouquet garni (see below)
500g (1lb) fresh tagliatelle
salt and freshly ground pepper
freshly grated Parmesan cheese, to serve

Bouquet garni *To make a fresh bouquet garni, sandwich a sprig of fresh thyme or oregano, 1 bay leaf and 1 crushed parsley stalk between two 4 cm (1½ in) sticks of celery and secure with string.*

❶ Finely slice the celery. Finely chop the shallots. Remove the rind and cut the bacon into strips. Crush the garlic.

❷ Heat the olive oil in a saucepan, add the shallots and fry until translucent. Add the celery and continue cooking for 1 minute. Add the beef and cook until browned, stirring occasionally. Add the bacon and garlic and cook for a further 2–3 minutes before adding the wine.

❸ Drain the chopped tomatoes in a sieve, reserving the juice. Add the drained tomatoes and stir the mixture. Add the tomato purée, vinegar, Worcestershire sauce, sugar and Tabasco and simmer gently for 4 minutes, then add the reserved tomato juice, beef stock and bouquet garni. Season well with salt and pepper. Leave to simmer.

❹ Meanwhile, cook the pasta in a large pan of boiling water according to the instructions on the packet.

❺ When cooked, drain the pasta well. Stir a little of the Bolognese sauce into the pasta to flavour, and serve the remaining sauce on top. Discard the bouquet garni. Serve with Parmesan cheese.

Madeira Steak with Rosti

SERVES 2

*You could make your own beef stock – but that's time-consuming – or use
cubes or granules, but by far the best is beef stock sold in cartons.*

225g (8oz) Cyprus potatoes
2 teaspoons mixed peppercorns
two 100g (4oz) fillet steaks
100g (4oz) unsalted butter
1 small garlic clove
75g (3oz) chestnut mushrooms
2 teaspoons chopped flat-leaved fresh parsley
50ml (2fl oz) Madeira
50ml (2fl oz) red wine
225ml (8fl oz) beef stock
225g (8oz) tender young spinach leaves
salt and freshly ground black pepper

❶ Put the potatoes in a saucepan of cold salted water, bring to the boil and simmer for 8 minutes. Drain and, when cool enough to handle, remove the peel.

❷ Pre-heat the oven to 200°C/400°F/Gas 6.

❸ Heat a sauté or frying pan. Crush the peppercorns and use them to season both sides of the steaks. Add a knob of the butter to the pan and heat until turning golden. Add the steaks and seal them quickly on both sides until browned. Transfer to a baking tray and place in the oven for 8 minutes.

❹ Finely chop the garlic. Slice the mushrooms. Add the garlic, mushrooms and parsley to the pan and cook for 1–2 minutes until just tender. Add the Madeira and wine, scraping the bottom of the pan with a wooden spoon and boil until well reduced and syrupy.

❺ Grate the potatoes into a bowl and add 25g (1oz) of the butter. Season with salt and pepper and mix well together.

❻ Melt 50g (2oz) of the butter in a frying pan with two 10cm (4in) plain pastry cutters. Add the potato mixture to the cutters in the pan, pushing down with a spatula, and cook for 4–5 minutes until golden around the edges.

❼ Add the stock to the sauce and boil quickly to reduce by two-thirds.

❽ Remove the steaks from the oven and leave to rest. Turn the potato rosti and cook for a further 3–4 minutes.

❾ Cook the spinach in a pan, in just the water that clings to the leaves after washing, until wilted. Add a knob of butter and season with salt and pepper.

❿ Add any juices from the steaks to the sauce, season and whisk in the remaining butter but do not let it boil. Spread the spinach in the middle of warmed serving plates. Press the rosti out of the cutters and place on top, followed by the steak. Spoon around the sauce and serve.

Steak au Poivre

SERVES 2

Of all the cuts of beef, fillet is the most expensive. This is because it is, without doubt, the tenderest and cooks beautifully. You could use rump or sirloin as an alternative and that would give you a little saving.

groundnut oil, for deep-frying
two 225g (8oz) Maris Piper potatoes
1 tablespoon black peppercorns
two 100g (4oz) fillet steaks
25g (1oz) butter, plus a knob
2 tablespoons sunflower oil
100g (4oz) frozen petit pois
½ teaspoon sugar
about 2 tablespoons brandy
420ml (4fl oz) double cream
salt

1 Pre-heat the oven to 200°C/400°F/Gas 6. Heat the oil in a pan for deep-frying to 190°C/375°F (check with a thermometer).

2 Peel the potatoes and cut into thick chips and dry in a tea-towel. Add the chips to the oil and fry for 6–7 minutes until just starting to colour. Remove and drain on kitchen paper.

3 Heat a heavy-based frying pan. Coarsely crush the peppercorns, sprinkle over both sides of the steaks and press hard to cover. Add the 25g (1oz) of butter and the sunflower oil to the pan and fry the steaks for 2 minutes on each side, then reduce the heat and continue to cook to taste. Season with salt.

4 Meanwhile, check the heat of the oil and return the chips to the pan for 2–3 minutes until crisp and golden. Drain well on kitchen paper and season with salt.

5 Put the petit pois in a small saucepan of boiling salted water and cook for about 5 minutes until just tender. Drain and toss in a knob of butter and the sugar.

6 Remove the steaks from the pan and keep warm on serving plates. Add the brandy to the pan and set alight. Stir in the cream and heat gently. Pour the sauce over the steaks and serve with the chips and petit pois.

Spicy Beef with Thai Jasmine Rice and Crispy Noodles

SERVES 2

It is the cornflour in this recipe that binds together the ingredients and gives the beef its spiciness. For best results, the beef should be sliced as thinly as possible.

225g (8oz) lean rump steak
1 tablespoon light soy sauce
1 tablespoon dry sherry
1 tablespoon hoisin sauce
2 tablespoons cornflour
150g (5oz) Thai jasmine rice
vegetable oil, for deep-frying
25g (1oz) bean thread noodles (see below)
100g (4oz) broccoli
1 red pepper
2 tablespoons chopped fresh coriander
FOR THE SAUCE
4 tablespoons dry sherry
3 tablespoons light soy sauce
1 teaspoon sesame oil
1 tablespoon clear honey
1 teaspoon hot chilli sauce
salt and freshly ground black pepper

Bean thread noodles *are also known as cellophane or transparent noodles. They are made from mung beans and come in long strands which are folded over for packaging.*

1 Slice the beef into thin strips and put in a bowl with the soy sauce, sherry, hoisin sauce and cornflour. Mix well and set aside.

2 Cook the rice according to the packet instructions.

3 Meanwhile, heat 7.5cm (3in) of vegetable oil in a wok. Add the noodles and cook for 1 minute until puffed up and white. Using a slotted spoon, remove from the wok and drain on kitchen paper. Remove the wok from the heat and allow to cool.

4 Cut the broccoli into very small florets. Cut the pepper in half, remove the core and seeds and very thinly slice the flesh.

5 Stir together all the sauce ingredients.

6 Drain the oil from the wok into a large bowl or jug, leaving a thin coating in the wok. Return the wok to a high heat, add the beef and stir-fry for 1 minute until sealed on all sides. Add the broccoli and pepper and cook for 2 minutes. Add the sauce and cook for a further 2 minutes. Add salt and pepper to taste and stir in the chopped coriander.

7 Divide the cooked rice between 2 warmed serving plates and spoon the spicy beef mixture over it. Top with the crispy noodles and serve at once.

Creamy Dijon Beef with Bubble and Squeak

SERVES 2

Covering meat with clingfilm or greaseproof paper when flattening it out prevents the flesh from tearing. You could also use a plastic bag.

350g (12oz) potatoes
2 rump steaks, trimmed
1 tablespoon Dijon mustard
25g/1oz butter, softened
2 tablespoons chopped fresh chervil
1 teaspoon black peppercorns
3 tablespoons olive oil
150ml (¼ pint) double cream
4 Savoy cabbage leaves
1 shallot
150ml (¼ pint) red wine
a pinch of sugar
salt and freshly ground black pepper

1 Peel and dice the potatoes and put in a large saucepan of cold salted water. Bring to the boil and cook for 6–8 minutes until tender.

2 Meanwhile, place the steaks on a sheet of clingfilm or greaseproof paper. Cover each with another sheet and bat out with a rolling pin until very thin (about 0.5cm/¼in thick).

3 In a small bowl, mix together the mustard, butter and chopped chervil. Crush the peppercorns in a pestle and mortar then mix into the mustard butter with a little salt. Spread the mixture on to the steaks and roll up tightly. Tie string around the rolls to secure.

4 Heat 1 tablespoon of oil in a frying pan.

Add the steaks and cook for 8 minutes, turning frequently until well browned.

5 Drain the potatoes and mash well until smooth. Stir in 2–3 tablespoons of the cream and add salt and pepper to taste.

6 Remove the thick centre stalks from the cabbage leaves and roll up the leaves tightly. Slice across the rolls to shred the cabbage. Cook the cabbage in a pan of boiling salted water for 2 minutes until just tender. Drain well and mix with the potatoes.

7 Heat the remaining oil in a frying pan. Add the bubble and squeak mixture and cook for 3–4 minutes until a crust forms on the bottom. Break up the mixture and cook for a further 3 minutes until a crust forms again.

8 Meanwhile, remove the steaks from the pan and place in a warmed roasting tin. Cover with foil and rest for 3–4 minutes.

9 Finely chop the shallot. Add to the steak pan and cook for 2 minutes until beginning to soften. Add the red wine and boil rapidly for 1 minute. Stir in the remaining cream and add sugar, salt and pepper to taste.

10 Cut the steak rolls in half. Spoon the bubble and squeak on to warmed serving plates and arrange the steak rolls on top. Spoon around the creamy sauce and serve at once.

Sweet and Sour Pork

SERVES 2

Get the oil in the wok very hot before adding the food and remember to keep the ingredients on the move once inside the pan.

175g (6oz) piece of pork fillet
1 small onion
1 small carrot
50g (2oz) baby sweetcorn
1 small red pepper
2 spring onions
50g (2oz) mange-tout peas
2 tablespoons sunflower oil
1 tablespoon sugar
120ml (4fl oz) chicken stock
2 tablespoons white wine vinegar
2 tablespoons tomato ketchup
1 teaspoon cornflour (optional)
225g (8oz) cooked long grain rice
25g (1oz) unsalted cashew nuts
25g (1oz) frozen petit pois, thawed
1 egg, beaten
2 tablespoons light soy sauce
salt and freshly ground black pepper

❶ Cut the pork into thin strips. Thickly slice the onion. Peel and thinly slice the carrot diagonally. Cut the sweetcorn into diagonal pieces. Cut both ends off the pepper, remove the seeds and slice the flesh into 2.5cm (1in) strips, then cut into diamonds. Finely chop the spring onions. Cut the mange-tout in half.

❷ Heat a wok with 1 tablespoon of oil until very hot. Season the pork with salt and pepper and toss in the sugar. Add to the wok and stir-fry for 1–2 minutes until caramelised to a rich golden colour. Remove with a slotted spoon and drain in a sieve, standing over a bowl.

❸ Meanwhile, put the stock, vinegar and tomato ketchup in a small saucepan and bring to the boil. Simmer until thickened and reduced, adding the cornflour, mixed with a little cold water, to thicken the sauce if necessary.

❹ Add the onion to the wok and stir-fry for 1 minute. Add the carrot and sweetcorn and cook for 2 minutes.

❺ Heat the remaining oil in a frying pan. Add the rice, nuts and petit pois and stir-fry for 1 minute. Add the spring onions and cook for a further 1–2 minutes, tossing occasionally.

❻ Add the pepper and mange-tout to the wok and cook for 2 minutes.

❼ Pour the egg, in a thin stream, into the rice mixture, stirring all the time. Sprinkle over the soy sauce and remove from the heat.

❽ Stir the sweet and sour sauce into the vegetables until coated. Add the pork and stir-fry for 2–3 minutes until tender.

❾ Spoon the rice on to warmed serving plates and arrange the pork mixture on top. Serve at once with chopsticks.

Big Soup with Pesto Grills

SERVES 2

This is a real winter warmer, with a distinct taste of the Mediterranean from the pesto.

1 small onion
100g (4oz) rindless back bacon rashers
8 tablespoons olive oil
1 small carrot
1 celery stick
300ml (½ pint) hot vegetable stock
400g (14oz) can chopped tomatoes
50g (2oz) pasta shells
25g (1oz) unsalted cashew nuts
50g (2oz) piece of Parmesan cheese
a bunch of fresh basil leaves
1 small garlic clove
1 small French baguette
3 Savoy cabbage leaves
1 small courgette
salt and freshly ground black pepper

❶ Finely chop the onion. Cut the bacon into strips. Heat 2 tablespoons of the oil in a large saucepan. Add the onion and bacon and cook for 5 minutes until golden.

❷ Peel and cut the carrot into batons. Slice the celery on the diagonal. Add to the pan, stirring to coat, and cook for 1 minute. Pour in the stock and tomatoes and add the pasta. Cover and simmer for 8–10 minutes until the pasta is just tender.

❸ Heat a small frying pan and dry-fry the cashew nuts until toasted.

❹ Meanwhile, grate 25g (1oz) of the Parmesan cheese and roughly tear the basil leaves. Put the cheese, basil, the remaining oil, the garlic, nuts, salt and pepper in a food processor or blender and whiz to form a purée. Spoon the pesto sauce into a bowl.

❺ Cut the baguette into slices and arrange on a baking tray. Grill on both sides until lightly toasted.

❻ Remove the thick stalks from the cabbage leaves and place the leaves on top of each other. Roll up like a cigar and shred into thin ribbons. Stir into the pasta pan and continue to cook. Cut the courgette into fingers, add to the pan and continue to cook.

❼ Spread some of the pesto on one side of the toasts and grill for a further minute.

❽ When the pasta is cooked, season with salt and pepper to taste. Stir some of the pesto into the soup to taste and ladle into bowls. Scatter over shavings of the remaining Parmesan cheese and serve with the pesto grills and remaining pesto in a ramekin dish.

To make parmesan shavings *use a vegetable peeler with a U-shaped handle and a swivel blade and shred long shavings from a piece of cheese directly on to the dish just before serving.*

Toad-in-the-Holes with Onion Gravy and Vichy Carrots

SERVES 2

Another sure-fire winter warmer, this is a super recipe which the younger members of your family are certain to love. It's easy to follow, fun to cook and great to eat!

a little dripping or oil
50g (2oz) plain flour
1 egg
150ml (¼ pint) whole-fat milk and water, mixed
2 cooked pork sausages
1 small onion
25g (1oz) butter
200g (7oz) carrots
a pinch of sugar
1 tablespoon chopped fresh parsley
4 medium mushrooms
25ml (1fl oz) red wine
150ml (¼ pint) beef stock
salt and freshly ground black pepper

❶ Pre-heat the oven to 220°C/425°F/Gas 7. Put the dripping in the bottom of 2 sections of a Yorkshire pudding tin and put in the oven to heat until the tin is hot and smoking.

❷ Meanwhile, sift the flour and a pinch of salt into a bowl. Make a well in the centre and break the egg into the centre. Pour the water and milk mixture into the centre and whisk the liquid and egg into the flour. Beat well until smooth and lump-free.

❸ Slice the sausages. Pour the batter into the 2 sections of the tin. Put the sausage slices in the middle and bake in the oven for 8–10 minutes, until well risen and golden.

❹ To make the onion gravy, finely slice the onion. Melt half the butter in a saucepan. Add the onion and fry until golden, stirring occasionally.

❺ Peel the carrots and put in a pan with 50ml (2fl oz) water, the sugar and the remaining butter. Bring to the boil and boil until the water has evaporated. Stir in the parsley and season with salt and pepper.

❻ Slice the mushrooms. Stir the onions, add the red wine, stock and mushrooms and bring to the boil. Simmer for a few minutes until the mushrooms are soft.

❼ Serve the toad-in-the-holes, as soon as they are cooked, with the onion gravy and Vichy carrots.

Bacon and Colcannon with Cider Sauce

SERVES 2

If you are unable to obtain spring greens use fresh spinach or rocket leaves.

350g (12oz) floury potatoes
50g (2oz) spring greens
2 teaspoons English mustard powder
2 teaspoons demerara sugar
200ml (7fl oz) dry cider
4 bacon chops or 2 gammon steaks
1 tablespoon sunflower oil
25g (1oz) butter
1 tablespoon plain flour
2 spring onions
50ml (2fl oz) milk
1 whole nutmeg, for grating
3 cherry tomatoes
½ teaspoon chopped fresh parsley
salt and freshly ground black pepper
sprigs of flat-leaved parsley, to garnish

1 Pre-heat the oven to 180°C/350°F/Gas 4.

2 Peel and dice the potatoes. Put in a saucepan of cold salted water, bring to the boil and simmer for 6–8 minutes until tender.

3 Strip the spring greens from the stems and shred the leaves. Steam for 2–3 minutes, then remove from the heat.

4 Mix together the mustard, sugar and 2 teaspoons of the cider to make a smooth sauce. Spread over both sides of the bacon chops or gammon steaks.

5 Heat the oil and a knob of the butter in a frying pan. Add the chops or steaks and cook for 1–2 minutes on each side until well glazed. Transfer to a baking dish and place in the oven for 10–15 minutes to finish cooking.

6 Stir the flour into the pan and cook for 1 minute, stirring. Gradually whisk in the remaining cider and simmer for 2–3 minutes until smooth, stirring occasionally.

7 Finely chop the spring onions and put in a small pan with the milk. Grate in a little nutmeg and slowly bring to the boil then simmer for 2–3 minutes.

8 Drain the potatoes. Mash them until smooth, beat in the flavoured milk and a knob of the butter. Stir in the spring greens.

9 Heat a small frying pan. Cut the tomatoes in half. Add to the pan, with the cut sides facing down, and cook over a high heat until they are lightly golden. Turn over and remove from the heat. Season with salt and pepper and sprinkle with the chopped parsley.

10 Pile the colcannon on to warmed serving plates. Add the chops or steaks and spoon over the sauce. Garnish with the tomatoes and parsley sprigs and serve.

Colcannon *is a popular Irish dish made from potatoes and cooked vegetables. It can be flavoured with herbs and may be fried.*

Roast Pork with Apple Sauté

SERVES 2

As a young boy, roast pork was the first thing I cooked. It looked lovely but as it was carved it oozed blood. Always check that pork is cooked through.

3 tablespoons sunflower oil
50g (2oz) unsalted butter
1 teaspoon dried rosemary
1 tablespoon Dijon mustard
1 tablespoon light muscovado sugar
1 tablespoon honey
juice of ½ a lemon
225g (8oz) tenderloin of pork
150ml (¼ pint) cider
150ml (¼ pint) chicken stock
10 waxy baby new potatoes
2 carrots
2 courgettes
1 small eating apple
1 teaspoon arrowroot
salt and freshly ground black pepper

1 Pre-heat the oven to 220°C/450°F/Gas 8 and place a roasting tin in the oven.

2 Heat 1 tablespoon of the oil and 15g (½ oz) of the butter in a frying pan. In a shallow dish, mix together the rosemary, mustard, sugar, honey and lemon juice. Cut the pork in half and add to the dish, turning to coat. Shake off any excess marinade and add the pork to the pan. Cook over a high heat for 2–3 minutes on each side to seal.

3 Transfer the pork to the roasting tin and bake in the oven for 10–12 minutes or until tender.

4 Add the cider to the pan with any remaining marinade, then add the stock and boil until reduced by half.

5 Cut a slice off the top and bottom of each potato, then put the potatoes in a saucepan of cold salted water. Bring to the boil then cook for 5 minutes.

6 Peel the carrots. Using a food processor or by hand, cut the courgettes and carrots into thin slices.

7 Heat the remaining 40g (1½oz) of the butter in a small frying pan. Drain the potatoes and add to the pan. Cover with a round of greaseproof paper and then a lid and cook for 5 minutes on each side until golden.

8 Core, halve and thinly slice the apple. Heat the remaining oil in a wok. Add the apple, vegetables, salt and pepper. Stir-fry over a high heat until lightly golden.

9 Remove the pork from the oven and leave to rest. Pour any juices into the cider sauce. Blend a little water with the arrowroot to slacken it, add to the sauce and cook for 1–2 minutes until thickened, stirring.

10 Place the vegetables on warmed serving plates. Carve the pork and place on top. Pour over the sauce, arrange the potatoes around the edge and serve.

Pork and Noodle Soup with Sesame Prawn Toasts

SERVES 2

I hate sesame prawn toast nearly as much as I hate chocolate. The reason is simple: I am unable to resist them. You won't believe just how lovely this dish is.

2 tablespoons dark soy sauce
1 teaspoon clear honey
75g (3oz) boneless loin pork chop
2 tablespoons sunflower oil
100g (4oz) cooked, peeled prawns
2.5cm (1in) cube of fresh root ginger, frozen (see page 31)
1 egg white
1 teaspoon cornflour
2 slices of medium-thick white bread
2 tablespoons sesame seeds
groundnut oil, for deep frying
25g (1oz) button mushrooms
1 red chilli
2 garlic cloves
900ml (1½ pints) hot chicken stock
50g (2oz) instant chicken-flavoured Chinese noodles
2 spring onions
75g (3oz) spring greens
25g (1oz) bamboo shoots
salt and freshly ground black pepper

1 Mix together 1 tablespoon of the soy sauce and the honey. Pour over the pork and turn in the marinade. Heat a frying pan with 1 tablespoon of the sunflower oil. Fry the pork for about 4 minutes each side or until lightly caramelised and golden brown.

2 Put the prawns in a food processor. Remove the ginger from the freezer then peel and grate and add half to the prawns. Season with a good pinch of salt. Add the egg white and cornflour and process until the prawns are well minced.

3 Spread the prawn mixture on the bread slices and cover with the sesame seeds, pressing them gently into the prawns. Cut off and discard the crusts.

4 Heat the oil for deep-frying in a wok. Deep-fry the prawn toasts, sesame seed side down (stand well back as the fat will spit a little) for 1 minute, then turn over and cook for about another 30 seconds. Using a slotted spoon, lift out and drain on kitchen paper.

5 Slice the mushrooms. Finely chop the chilli, discarding the seeds and chop the garlic. Heat the remaining sunflower oil in a large saucepan. Add the mushrooms, chilli and garlic to the pan with the remaining ginger and fry for about 30 seconds. Add the stock and noodles and bring to the boil.

6 Remove the pork from the frying pan and leave to cool a little.

7 Finely slice the spring onions. Shred the spring greens and add to the boiling stock with the spring onions. Season with the remaining soy sauce, and pepper and stir in the bamboo shoots.

8 Slice the pork into thin strips and stir into the soup. Simmer, if necessary, until the noodles are tender.

9 To serve, ladle the soup into large

bowls, cut the prawn toasts into triangles and serve with the soup.

••

Ginger *If you keep a piece of peeled, fresh ginger in the freezer, you will find it much easier to grate just before adding it to a dish.*

Cheesy Macaroni, Ham and Veggie Bake

SERVES 2

Comfort food, that's what this is, and for the reluctant cook it's ideal. A no-nonsense recipe that produces a really good nutritious meal with very little effort.

150g (5oz) quick-cook macaroni
1 small leek
75g (3oz) piece of cooked ham
2 teaspoons sunflower oil
75g (3oz) cauliflower
75g (3oz) broccoli
25g (1oz) butter
25g (1oz) plain flour
450ml (¾ pint) milk
½ teaspoon English prepared mustard
¼ teaspoon paprika
50g (2oz) Cheddar cheese
1 chicory head
a handful of watercress
1 small red eating apple
a few walnut halves
3 tablespoons walnut oil
1 tablespoon lemon juice
salt and freshly ground black pepper

1 Cook the macaroni in boiling salted water for 5 minutes or according to the packet instructions.

2 Meanwhile, slice the leek and cut the ham into 2cm (¾ in) strips. Heat a small frying pan and add the oil. Add the leek and ham to the pan and stir.

3 Cut the cauliflower and broccoli into small florets of the same size and cook both in a saucepan of boiling water for 4–5 minutes.

4 Meanwhile, make a white sauce. Melt the butter in a pan, add the flour and cook for 20 seconds. Remove from the heat and gradually stir in the milk to produce a smooth sauce. Slowly bring to the boil and continue to cook, stirring over a low heat, until the sauce thickens. Ladle a little water from the cauliflower and broccoli and add to the sauce to thin, if necessary. Add the mustard, paprika, salt and pepper. Grate most of the cheese into the sauce and whisk until smooth.

5 Pre-heat the grill. Drain the vegetables. Remove the leeks and the ham from the heat and tip into a large bowl. Drain the macaroni. Add the macaroni and cheese sauce to the vegetables, stir to combine and then pile into a flameproof dish. Grate the remaining cheese over the top. Place on a baking tray and grill until bubbling.

6 Meanwhile, make the salad. Peel the leaves away from the chicory and place in a bowl. Add the watercress. Cut the apple into slices and add with the walnuts.

7 To make the dressing, put the walnut oil, lemon juice, salt and pepper in a screw-top jar and shake until well combined. Carefully fold into the salad. Serve the salad with the cheesy macaroni.

Pork Goulash

SERVES 2

Stew-based dishes are even nicer when reheated and served the next day. Cook quickly, store in a fridge and then reheat thoroughly.

1 small red onion
1 small red pepper
1 tablespoon sunflower oil
25g (1oz) butter
1 large garlic clove
50g (2oz) button mushrooms
225g (8oz) pork tenderloin, well trimmed
2 teaspoons hot paprika, plus extra for dusting
1 tablespoon plain flour
150ml (¼ pint) chicken stock
200g (7oz) can chopped tomatoes
175g (6oz) fresh tagliatelle
1 teaspoon poppy seeds
a small bunch of flat-leaved fresh parsley
about 4 tablespoons soured cream
salt and freshly ground black pepper

1 Chop the onion. Cut the pepper in half, discard the core and seeds, and finely chop the flesh. Heat the oil and half the butter in a sauté or large frying pan. Add the onion and pepper and stir to coat. Crush the garlic with some salt, add to the pan and continue to cook over a high heat for 2–3 minutes until softened. Slice the mushrooms and add to the pan, stirring to coat.

2 Cut the pork into 4cm (1½in) long strips and add to the pan, stirring to coat and continue to cook until lightly browned.

3 Stir the 2 teaspoons of paprika and the flour into the pan and cook for 1 minute, stirring. Season with salt and pepper to taste. Pour in the stock and add the tomatoes. Bring to the boil, then simmer for about 5 minutes until the meat is tender.

4 Meanwhile, plunge the tagliatelle in a

Vegetable
Lasagne
(page 58)

Kofta Kebabs
with Houmous
Sauce and
Couscous Salad
(page 14)

Seared Trout
Fillets with
Warm Salad
Niçoise
(page 72)

Chimichangas
(page 40)

Spicy Beef with Thai Jasmine Rice and Crispy Noodles *(page 23)*

Florentine Puffs with Mixed Bean Salad *(page 59)*

Parmesan Chicken with Tomato Tagliatelle *(page 42)*

Roast Pork with Apple Sauté *(page 29)*

Marmalade
Duck with
Celeriac
Purée
(page 50)

WON'T
OK

Chicken and
Cranberry
Twists
(page 39)

**Mediterranean
Lamb and
Vegetable
Platter
(page 12)**

**Pan-Fried
Salmon and
Watercress
Sauce
(page 64)**

Basket of Chocolate Praline with Mango Sauce *(page 87)*

Pan-Fried Bread and Butter Puddings *(page 91)*

**Poached Pears
in Red Wine
(page 84)**

**Crêpes
Suzette
(page 88)**

pan of boiling salted water and cook for 1–2 minutes until just tender. Drain the tagliatelle and toss in the remaining butter and the poppy seeds.

5 Chop the parsley and stir into the pork.

6 Arrange the tagliatelle on warmed serving plates, making a slight dip in the centre and spoon in the pork mixture. Add a dollop of soured cream and sprinkle over a little more paprika. Serve at once.

Spring Stew with Pork, Orange and Beetroot

SERVES 2

In this recipe it is necessary to toss the cubes of pork in flour prior to cooking them. This will protect the meat during the sealing process and the flour will help to give body to the finished sauce.

1 onion
1 garlic clove
olive oil, for frying
1 tablespoon plain flour
½ teaspoon ground cinnamon
250g (9oz) lean pork
juice of 2 oranges
150ml (¼ pint) dry cider
1 tablespoon white wine vinegar
a sprig of fresh thyme
2 slices of medium-thick white bread
100g (4oz) cooked fresh beetroot
400g (14oz) can cannellini beans, drained
salt and freshly ground black pepper
crusty bread, to serve

1 Slice the onion and garlic. Heat 2 tablespoons of oil in a saucepan. Add the onion and garlic and cook for 3–4 minutes until golden.

2 Mix together the flour, cinnamon and a little salt and pepper. Dice the pork and toss the cubes in the flour to coat then add to the pan. Cook for 2–3 minutes, stirring, until well browned. Add the orange juice, cider, vinegar and thyme. Bring to the boil, cover and cook for 5 minutes.

3 Meanwhile, heat 2–3 tablespoons of oil in a frying pan. Cut the crusts off the bread then cut into triangles. Add to the pan and fry until lightly golden. Drain on kitchen paper.

4 Dice the beetroot and add to the stew with the cannellini beans. Cover and cook for 5 minutes until the meat is tender. Add salt and pepper to taste. Serve with crusty bread.

Beetroot Buy cooked fresh beetroot for this recipe, not those preserved in vinegar in jars.

POULTRY
DISHES

Italian Chicken with Tomato-Crusted Potatoes *35*

Speedy Coq au Vin *36*

Fragrant Chicken Biryani *37*

Cheat's Roast Chicken with Bacon, Roast Potatoes, Bread Sauce and Mustard Cabbage *38*

Chicken and Cranberry Twists *39*

Chimichangas *40*

Chicken Satay with Quick Fried Cabbage *41*

Parmesan Chicken with Tomato Tagliatelle *42*

Chicken and Leek Pie *43*

Creamy Tarragon Chicken *44*

Ricotta Chicken Pockets with Braised Lentils *45*

Turkey Saltimbocca with Spinach and Olive Oil Mash *46*

Chinese Chow Mein *47*

Sesame Turkey and Garlic Fried Rice *48*

Coronation Turkey *49*

Marmalade Duck with Celeriac Purée *50*

Italian Chicken with Tomato-Crusted Potatoes

SERVES 2

Marinating meat or poultry allows it to absorb whatever ingredients, flavours and spices you wish it to take on, giving it an intense flavour.

two 100g (4oz) boneless chicken
breasts, skinned

1 garlic clove

4 tablespoons olive oil

3 teaspoons sun-dried tomato purée

1 teaspoon Dijon mustard

1 onion

225g (8oz) cooked new potatoes

150ml (¼ pint) white wine

4 tablespoons crème fraiche

a squeeze of lemon juice

1 tablespoon snipped fresh chives

100g (4oz) spinach leaves

a knob of butter

pinch of freshly grated nutmeg

salt and freshly ground black pepper

❶ Slash the chicken breasts and set aside. Chop the garlic. In a shallow dish, mix together half the olive oil, 1 teaspoon of the sun-dried tomato purée, the mustard, half the garlic, salt and pepper. Add the chicken, stir, and set aside to marinate.

❷ Chop the onion. Heat the remaining oil in a frying pan. Add half the onion and cook until softened and lightly browned at the edges. Quarter the potatoes, add to the pan and cook until golden, turning occasionally. Stir in the remaining sun-dried tomato purée and just heat through. Keep warm.

❸ Heat the frying pan. Add the chicken breasts and cook for 10–15 minutes until cooked through, turning occasionally. Remove from the pan and keep warm.

❹ Add the remaining onion and garlic to the pan and cook gently for 3–5 minutes until the onion has softened. Pour in the wine and cook until reduced by half. Stir in the crème fraiche, add the lemon juice and simmer for 2–3 minutes until slightly thickened. Season with salt and pepper to taste and stir in the chives.

❺ Wash the spinach and remove the stalks. Put in a pan with just the water that clings to the leaves after washing. Add the butter and cook until wilted. Season to taste, add the nutmeg and drain off any excess liquid.

❻ To serve, arrange the chicken on warmed serving plates. Add the potatoes and the spinach and drizzle around some of the sauce. Serve at once.

Speedy Coq au Vin

SERVES 2

The sauce in this recipe is thickened with a 'beurre manié'. This is simply a mixture of flour and butter which is added, in small quantities, to a hot liquid until the required consistency has been achieved.

350g (12oz) potatoes
1 tablespoon sunflower oil
4 boneless chicken thighs, skinned
50g (2oz) rindless streaky bacon
100g (4oz) button onions
50g (2oz) chestnut mushrooms
1 garlic clove
300ml (½ pint) red wine
1 tablespoon tomato purée
1 teaspoon fresh thyme leaves
1 bay leaf
25g (1oz) butter, softened
1 tablespoon plain flour
2 tablespoons milk
1 tablespoon roughly chopped fresh parsley
salt and freshly ground black pepper
sprigs of thyme and bay leaves, to garnish

❶ Peel the potatoes and cut them into 2cm (¾in) cubes. Put in a saucepan of cold salted water, bring to the boil and cook for 8 minutes until tender.

❷ Heat the oil in a frying pan. Add the chicken and fry for 4 minutes, turning once, until the chicken is golden.

❸ Meanwhile, cut the bacon widthways into thin strips. Add the onions and bacon to the pan and cook for 3 minutes.

❹ Meanwhile, cut the mushrooms into quarters and crush the garlic. Add to the pan and cook for 2 minutes. Stir in the wine, tomato purée, thyme leaves, bay leaf, salt and pepper. Bring to the boil then simmer for 8 minutes, stirring occasionally, until the chicken is tender and cooked through.

❺ Put 15g (½oz) of the butter in a bowl, add the flour and mix to a smooth paste.

❻ Drain the potatoes and return to the pan. Add the remaining 15g (½oz) butter, the milk, salt and pepper and mash until smooth and fluffy. Stir in the parsley.

❼ Using a slotted spoon, lift the chicken, onions and mushrooms out of the pan and keep hot. Add the butter and flour paste to the cooking liquid and bring to the boil, whisking all the time, until thickened. Simmer for 1 minute. Return the chicken, onions and mushrooms to the red wine sauce and stir until coated.

❽ Spoon the chicken and red wine sauce on to warmed serving plates and serve with the mashed potatoes. Garnish with sprigs of thyme and bay leaves.

Fragrant Chicken Biryani

SERVES 2

The raita is a refreshing accompaniment to the biryani and cools down the palate.

25g (1oz) butter
sunflower oil, for frying
2 shallots
2 garlic cloves
2 boneless chicken breasts, skinned
2 tablespoons biryani or medium curry paste
300ml (½ pint) chicken stock
150ml (¼ pint) natural yogurt
1 tablespoon sugar
2 tablespoons raisins
225g (8oz) basmati rice, well rinsed and drained
2 tablespoons flaked almonds
2 plum tomatoes
7.5cm (3in) piece of cucumber
1 lime
a small bunch of fresh mint
¼ teaspoon cayenne
10 uncooked mini poppadoms
salt and freshly ground black pepper

❶ Heat the butter and 1 tablespoon of the oil in a sauté or large frying pan. Chop the shallots and garlic and add to the pan. Cook for about 2 minutes.

❷ Using a pair of scissors, cut the chicken diagonally into thin slices. Add to the pan and stir-fry for 2 minutes until sealed.

❸ Add the curry paste and stir again for 2–3 seconds. Stir in the stock, yogurt, sugar and raisins. Season with salt and pepper to taste. Stir in the rice, cover tightly and cook for about 10 minutes, stirring occasionally, until all the liquid has been absorbed and the chicken is tender.

❹ Meanwhile, put the almonds in a small frying pan and dry-fry until toasted.

❺ Cut the tomatoes and cucumber into quarters and remove the seeds, then finely dice and place both in a small bowl. Cut the lime in half and squeeze half over the vegetables. Cut the remainder into wedges. Chop the mint and stir into the vegetables with the cayenne. Set the raita aside.

❻ Heat about 2.5cm (1in) of oil in a wok.

❼ Fry the poppadoms in batches for 5 seconds, until golden. Drain on kitchen paper.

❽ Pile the biryani on to warmed serving plates and garnish with the almonds and lime wedges. Arrange the poppadoms around the edge of the plates and spoon small mounds of the raita on each one. Serve at once.

Dry-frying, *in this recipe used to toast the almonds, does not involve the use of extra fat or oil. It is used to 'toast' nuts, 'roast' spices and fry fatty foods which release fat as they are heated and cooked.*

Cheat's Roast Chicken with Bacon, Roast Potatoes, Bread Sauce and Mustard Cabbage

SERVES 2

If you find the thought of preparing a complete main course daunting, just follow this recipe step-by-step and see just how easy it can be.

225g (8oz) potatoes
5 rashers of rindless streaky bacon
two 75g (3oz) chicken breasts, with skins on
2 tablespoons sunflower oil
6 pitted ready-to-eat prunes
a small bunch of fresh rosemary sprigs
8 cloves
1 shallot
6fl oz (175ml) milk
50g (2oz) day-old white breadcrumbs
25g (1oz) butter
3 tablespoons double cream
¼ Savoy cabbage
½ teaspoon wholegrain mustard
salt and freshly ground black pepper

1 Pre-heat the oven to 230°C/450°F/ Gas 8.

2 Peel and dice the potatoes. Put in a saucepan of cold salted water, cover, bring to the boil and par-boil for 5 minutes.

3 Using the back of a knife, stretch the bacon rashers. Make 3 slits in the skin side of each chicken breast. Cut 2 rashers of bacon into 3 equal lengths and place 1 in each slit. Season with salt and pepper. Heat 1 tablespoon of oil in a heavy-based frying pan and brown the chicken all over.

4 Place the chicken, skin-side down, in a roasting dish and roast in the oven for 12–15 minutes until tender.

5 Meanwhile, cut the remaining bacon rashers in half and wrap around the prunes, then add them to the chicken in the oven.

6 Drain the potatoes and add to the pan that the chicken was cooked in. Fry for about 5 minutes, adding a little chopped rosemary, until golden brown on all sides.

7 Meanwhile, stick the cloves in the shallot. Heat the milk with the shallot in a saucepan and bring to the boil, gradually stirring in the breadcrumbs. Season well and stir in half of the butter and 1 tablespoon of cream. Leave to rest. Discard the shallot.

8 Shred the cabbage. Heat a frying pan with a lid and add the remaining butter with 1 tablespoon water. Add the cabbage, cover and shake. When the cabbage begins to wilt add the remaining cream, the mustard, salt and pepper. Mix well together.

9 Put a chicken breast on each warmed serving plate with some of the potatoes, cabbage, bread sauce and 3 bacon rolls. Garnish with a sprig of rosemary and serve at once.

Chicken and Cranberry Twists

SERVES 2

These colourful little snacks are great fun to make and are especially nice to serve around Christmas. The potato dish is my favourite and I always make extra for the following day.

2 tablespoons olive oil
2 tablespoons Dijon mustard
1 tablespoon red wine vinegar
1 tablespoon clear honey
225g (8oz) chicken strips
100g (4oz) frozen cranberries, thawed
2 rashers of rindless streaky bacon
two 150g (5oz) potatoes, baked
50g (2oz) cream cheese
15g (½oz) butter
1 tablespoon chopped fresh parsley
1 tablespoon snipped fresh chives
1 small garlic clove
50g (2oz) caster sugar
grated rind and juice of 1 orange
salt and freshly ground black pepper
salad leaves, to serve.

❶ Pre-heat the oven to 200°C/400°F/Gas 6. Heat a griddle pan.

❷ Put the oil, mustard, vinegar and honey in a shallow non-metallic dish. Add the chicken strips and a handful of the cranberries and mix well together. Set aside to marinate.

❸ Place the bacon on the griddle pan and cook over a high heat until crispy. Cut the baked potatoes in half lengthways and scoop out the flesh, into a bowl, leaving a 5mm (¼in) border. Add the cream cheese, butter, parsley and chives to the bowl. Crush in the garlic and season with salt and pepper to taste. Remove the bacon from the griddle pan and crumble into the mixture. Mix well together. Pile the mixture into the potato shells and place in a roasting tin. Bake in the oven for about 10 minutes until heated through.

❹ Meanwhile, thread 2 chicken strips on to 15cm (6in) soaked bamboo skewers, interweaving them with 6 cranberries. Repeat with the remaining chicken. Place on the griddle pan and cook for 6–8 minutes until tender and golden, turning occasionally.

❺ Put the remaining cranberries in a small saucepan with the sugar, orange rind and juice and heat until bubbling and thickened, stirring all the time.

❻ Pre-heat the grill. Place the hot potatoes under a hot grill for 2–3 minutes until bubbling and lightly golden.

❼ Put the remaining marinade in a small pan and heat gently to make a warm dressing.

❽ Arrange the salad leaves on serving plates and drizzle over the marinade. Add 3 of the skewers and 2 potato halves to each. Serve at once with the cranberry relish.

Chimichangas

SERVES 2–3

This dish is perfect for someone who wants a tasty meal without too much effort. Treat your friends to a taste of Mexico.

1 small red onion
1 large garlic clove
sunflower oil, for frying
225g (8oz) stir-fry chicken pieces
1 tablespoon sun-dried tomato purée
½ teaspoon hot chilli powder
1 small red pepper
1 small courgette
100g (4oz) baby sweetcorn
6 tablespoons mild taco sauce
1 small avocado
2 plum tomatoes
2 spring onions
juice of 1 lime
6 tortillas
2 iceberg lettuce leaves
salt and freshly ground black pepper
soured cream, to serve

Tortillas *are eaten throughout Mexico and are a kind of pancake made from masa harina, a specially processed cornflour. In Mexico they are cooked on a griddle known as a comal, which is made of thin cast iron.*

❶ Chop the onion. Crush the garlic. Cut the chicken into 1 cm (½in) dice. Heat 2 tablespoons of the oil in a frying pan, add the onion and fry for 2–3 minutes until lightly golden. Add the garlic, chicken, tomato purée and chilli powder, stirring to coat. Continue to cook for 2–3 minutes, stirring occasionally.

❷ Cut the pepper in half, remove the core and seeds and dice the flesh. Dice the courgette, add to the pan with the pepper and mix well. Slice the sweetcorn and add to the pan. Stir-fry over a high heat for 3–4 minutes until the vegetables are completely tender and the chicken cooked through. Season well with salt and pepper.

❸ Tip into a bowl and stir in 4 tablespoons of the taco sauce. Leave to cool.

❹ Meanwhile, cut the avocado in half, remove the stone and skin and dice the flesh. Place in a bowl. Put the tomatoes in a bowl, cover with boiling water and leave for 30 seconds then plunge into cold water. Peel off the skins then dice the flesh, discarding the seeds. Add to the avocado. Finely chop the spring onions and add to the bowl with the remaining 2 tablespoons of the taco sauce and squeeze over the lime juice. Season and mix well together.

❺ Pre-heat a frying pan. Heat each tortilla in the dry pan for 20 seconds. Remove from the pan. Place 2 tablespoons of the cooled mixture in the centre of each. Fold the bottom up, sides in and top down to form a neat parcel. Secure with cocktail sticks. Make 6 parcels.

6 Heat about 4 tablespoons of the oil in the frying pan. Add the chimichangas, folded-side down, and fry for 5 minutes until golden, turning halfway through cooking. Drain on kitchen paper.

7 Shred the lettuce and arrange on serving plates with 2–3 of the chimichangas. Serve with the avocado salsa, soured cream and remaining taco sauce.

Chicken Satay with Quick Fried Cabbage

SERVES 2–3

You can buy wooden skewers from most good kitchen shops. Pre-soaking them in cold water prevents the chicken sticking to them.

½ a small onion
2 boned chicken breasts, skinned
1 teaspoon garlic purée
1½ teaspoons ginger purée
4 tablespoons soy sauce
½ teaspoon turmeric
3 tablespoons sunflower oil
juice of 1 lime
150g (5oz) fragrant Thai rice
100g (4oz) lightly salted, roasted peanuts
200ml (7fl oz) coconut cream
1½–2 teaspoons chilli sauce
1 teaspoon clear honey
½ a small white cabbage
½ red pepper
¼ stalk of lemon grass or ½ teaspoon dried
1 tablespoon chopped fresh coriander, plus sprigs to garnish
salt and freshly ground black pepper

1 Finely chop the onion. Cut the chicken into 1cm (½in) dice and put in a bowl. Mix the onion, garlic, ginger, soy sauce, turmeric and 2 tablespoons of the oil into the chicken, squeeze over the lime juice and leave to marinate for 30 minutes or longer if you have time.

2 Brush a ridged griddle pan with oil and pre-heat.

3 Thread the marinated chicken on to skewers and cook on the griddle for about 10 minutes on each side.

4 Meanwhile, put the rice into a saucepan of boiling water, season with salt and cook for 10 minutes.

5 Put the peanuts into a food processor and blend into fine crumbs. Tip the crumbs into a pan. Add 150ml (¼pint) of the coconut cream to the peanuts with the chilli sauce, honey and the marinade and heat gently, stirring occasionally.

⑥ Finely slice the white cabbage. Remove the core and seeds from the pepper and slice the flesh into thin strips. Heat the remaining 1 tablespoon of oil in a wok or large frying pan and stir-fry the cabbage and pepper for 3–4 minutes. Finely slice the lemon grass and add to the pan, with the remaining 50ml (2fl oz) of coconut cream. Season with salt and pepper and stir together. Add the chopped coriander.

⑦ Drain the rice and serve with the chicken satay and cabbage. Spoon a little of the peanut sauce on top of the chicken and garnish with coriander.

Parmesan Chicken with Tomato Tagliatelle

SERVES 2–3

If you are using fresh chicken breasts, rather than thawed frozen ones, you can double the ingredients and freeze two of the filled breasts.

50g (2oz) unsalted butter, softened
a sprig of fresh rosemary
1 garlic clove
15g (/½oz) freshly grated Parmesan cheese
25g (1oz) dried white breadcrumbs
two 100g (4oz) boneless chicken breasts, with skin on
about 4 tablespoons olive oil
1 large shallot
175g (6oz) tomato-flavoured tagliatelle
225g (8oz) mixed mushrooms, such as chestnut, oyster, shitake.
a small bunch of flat-leaved parsley
2 tablespoons Madeira or sweet sherry
salt and freshly ground black pepper

① Pre-heat the oven to 200°C/400°F/Gas 6.

② Put 25g (1oz) of the butter in a bowl. Finely chop the rosemary, crush the garlic and add both to the butter with the cheese and breadcrumbs. Season with salt and pepper to taste.

③ Heat a frying pan. Loosen the skin from the flesh of each chicken breast and spread the breadcrumb mixture on the flesh then smooth over the skin to cover the filling. Secure each with a cocktail stick.

④ Add a knob of the butter to the pan with 1 tablespoon of the oil. Add the chicken breasts skin-side down, and cook over a high heat for 2–3 minutes until golden, then turn and cook for a further 1–2 minutes.

⑤ Transfer the chicken to a roasting tin and bake for 10–12 minutes until tender.

⑥ Heat the frying pan again and add the remaining butter and a little of the oil. Slice the shallot and add to the pan. Reduce the heat and cook for 4–5 minutes until lightly golden.

⑦ Bring a large pan of salted water to the boil and plunge in the tagliatelle. Cook for 3–4 minutes for fresh (8–10 minutes for dried) until just tender.

⑧ Meanwhile, slice the mushrooms and finely chop the parsley. Add the mushrooms to the frying pan and cook for 3–4 minutes until just tender. Pour in the Madeira or sherry and allow to evaporate.

⑨ Drain the pasta and return to the pan. Add the mushroom mixture and the parsley and toss. Season with salt and pepper to taste and pour in enough oil to lightly coat the pasta.

⑩ Swirl some of the pasta on to warmed serving plates. Carve the chicken breasts diagonally into slices and fan out slightly. Serve at once with the pasta.

Chicken and Leek Pie

SERVES 2–3

It's crucial that dishes to be baked are placed in the oven when it is at the correct temperature, and not before, otherwise the cooking time will be incorrect and the pastry undercooked and soggy.

20cm (8in) square ready-rolled puff pastry, thawed if frozen

beaten egg, to glaze

2 small leeks

50g (2oz) butter

225g (8oz) boneless chicken breasts, skinned

75g (3oz) small chestnut mushrooms

1 tablespoon plain flour

150ml (¼ pint) chicken stock

2 large carrots

4 tablespoons crème fraiche

2 teaspoons Dijon mustard

½ teaspoon caster sugar

½ a lemon

1 tablespoon roughly chopped flat-leaved fresh parsley

salt and freshly ground black pepper

① Pre-heat the oven to 220°C/425°F/Gas 7.

② Cut a 2.5cm (1in) strip from round the edges of the pastry square. Brush the edges of the remaining square with egg, then place the strip around the edge of the remaining square to make a pastry case, trimming off the extra lengths. Prick the base and then brush all over with egg. Bake for 8 minutes until golden.

③ Meanwhile, heat a large frying pan. Slice the leeks on the diagonal. Add 25g (1oz) of the butter to the pan with the leeks and fry for 3–4 minutes until softened.

④ Cut the chicken into chunks and thickly slice the mushrooms. Add the chicken to the pan and stir-fry for 3–4 minutes until lightly browned. Add the mushrooms and cook for 1–2 minutes. Stir the flour into the pan with

43

the chicken, then gradually pour in the stock, stirring until smooth. Bring to the boil then simmer for 2 minutes, stirring occasionally.

5 Meanwhile, peel and thinly slice the carrots into ribbons. Heat a wok or large frying pan. Add the remaining butter to the wok and stir-fry the carrot ribbons for 1–2 minutes until just tender.

6 Remove the pastry case from the oven.

7 Stir the crème fraiche and mustard into the chicken mixture. Season with salt and pepper to taste and heat gently until warmed through.

8 Sprinkle the sugar over the carrots, add a squeeze of lemon juice and cook for 1–2 minutes. Toss the parsley with the carrots and season with pepper.

9 Remove the pastry case from the oven and spoon in the chicken mixture. Serve the pie with the carrots.

Creamy Tarragon Chicken
SERVES 2

When adding wine to a dish be sure to increase the heat and allow it to reduce. By boiling it you remove the alcohol and intensify the flavour.

100g (4oz) long-grain and wild rice mix
1 tablespoon olive oil
25g (1oz) unsalted butter
two 100g (4oz) boneless chicken breasts, skinned
1 small onion
175g (6oz) small button mushrooms
1 small garlic clove
50ml (2fl oz) white wine
150ml (¼ pint) chicken stock
150g (5oz) broccoli
4 sprigs of fresh tarragon
120ml (4fl oz) double cream
salt and freshly ground black pepper

1 Bring a large saucepan of boiling water to the boil and add the rice. Cook for 10–15 minutes until tender.

2 Meanwhile, add the oil and half the butter to a frying pan. Season the chicken all over with salt and pepper and add to the pan. Cook for 1–2 minutes, on each side, until lightly golden.

3 Finely chop the onion and add to the pan, stirring to coat. Cut the mushrooms into quarters, halve and crush the garlic with a little salt. Add both to the pan, stirring until well coated.

4 Pour in the wine (which should boil off very rapidly). Pour in the stock and boil for about 5 minutes until thickened and syrupy, turning the chicken occasionally.

5 Cut the broccoli into florets, add to a

pan of boiling salted water and cook for 3 minutes until just tender. Drain and toss in the remaining butter.

6 Remove the tarragon leaves from the stalks and snip with scissors. Add the cream to the pan with the chicken and cook until bubbling. Remove the chicken from the pan and keep warm. Continue to reduce the sauce until thickened, then stir in the tarragon and remove from the heat. Drain the rice. Carve each chicken breast into slices, fan out on a warmed serving plate and spoon the sauce over it. Serve at once with the rice and broccoli.

Ricotta Chicken Pockets with Braised Lentils

SERVES 2–3

This is in my top ten chicken dishes. The cheese simply oozes from the chicken and the green lentils are a lovely accompaniment.

25g (1oz) frozen chopped spinach, thawed and squeezed dry
75g (3oz) ricotta cheese
2 tablespoons freshly grated Parmesan cheese
a pinch of freshly grated nutmeg
two 100g (4oz) boneless chicken breasts, skinned
6 rashers of rindless streaky bacon
2 tablespoons olive oil
1 small carrot
1 celery stick
1 small onion
120ml (4fl oz) red wine
400g (14oz) can green lentils, drained
100g (4oz) mange-tout peas
25g (1oz) butter
1 small garlic clove
25g (1oz) fresh white breadcrumbs
salt and freshly ground black pepper

1 In a bowl, mix together the spinach, ricotta, Parmesan cheese and nutmeg. Using a sharp knife, make a deep slit through the thicker side of each chicken breast to make a pocket. Spoon in the ricotta mixture.

2 Using the back of a knife, stretch the bacon rashers. Wrap 3 rashers around each piece of chicken to enclose the filling completely.

3 Heat a large frying pan and add the oil. Add the chicken to the pan and seal on all sides.

4 Meanwhile, peel and dice the carrot and dice the celery. Finely chop the onion. Add the vegetables to the pan, stirring to coat. Reduce the heat and fry for 1 minute. Pour in the wine and lentils, cover and simmer for 8–10 minutes, turning occasionally, until the chicken is tender.

⑤ Put the mange-tout in a saucepan of boiling water and cook for 2–3 minutes.

⑥ Meanwhile, melt half the butter in a small frying pan. Crush the garlic and add to the pan with the breadcrumbs. Stir to coat completely in the butter and fry until golden. Season with salt and pepper to taste.

⑦ Drain the mange-tout, put on warmed serving plates and sprinkle with the crumbs.

⑧ Remove the chicken from the pan and increase the heat to evaporate any excess liquid. Slice the chicken and arrange on serving plates.

⑨ Whisk the remaining butter into the lentil mixture, spoon on to the plates and serve at once.

....

Ricotta is a soft Italian cheese made from the whey left over when producing other cheeses. It has a subtle flavour which makes it ideal for cooking.

Turkey Saltimbocca with Spinach and Olive Oil Mash

SERVES 2

A true saltimbocca is made using veal. Given the difficulty in some areas in obtaining this meat, turkey makes an ideal substitute. Don't be put off by the sound of olive oil mash. It's delightful and healthier than mash with butter.

1 large (225g/8oz) potato
2 turkey escalopes
3 slices of prosciutto ham
6 sage leaves
4 tablespoons olive oil
a small handful of pine kernels
100g (4oz) baby spinach leaves
50g (2oz) butter
1 large garlic clove
a squeeze of lemon juice
2 tablespoons freshly grated Parmesan cheese, plus shavings to garnish
2 cherry tomatoes
freshly ground black pepper

❶ Peel the potato and cut into small cubes. Put in a saucepan of cold salted water, bring to the boil and simmer for about 12 minutes until tender.

❷ Slice the turkey escalopes, at an angle, into 6 pieces. Place between 2 sheets of clingfilm or greaseproof paper and bash with a rolling pin until very thin.

❸ Season the turkey with pepper (do not add salt). Cut each slice of prosciutto in half lengthways making 6 strips. Wrinkle the strips of prosciutto until they fit on top of the pieces of turkey. Place a sage leaf on each and secure each with a cocktail stick.

④ Heat 1 tablespoon of olive oil in a frying pan. Fry the turkey pieces, prosciutto-side up, for 3 minutes then fry the other side for a further 3 minutes.

⑤ Meanwhile, heat a second frying pan and dry-fry the pine kernels (without any oil) until toasted. Tip them into the bowl.

⑥ Wash the spinach. Add the butter to the pan that the pine kernels were toasted in, add the spinach leaves, with only the water still clinging to the leaves after washing, and stir-fry until wilted. Meanwhile, chop the garlic and add to the spinach. Squeeze some lemon juice over the turkey.

⑦ Drain the potatoes then mash with 2 tablespoons of olive oil, the grated Parmesan cheese and the spinach mixture.

⑧ To serve, slice the tomatoes and arrange on serving plates. Add a spoonful of the mash. Remove the cocktail sticks and pile the turkey on top of the potatoes. Sprinkle with the pine kernels. Drizzle olive oil around the edge of the plates and place a few shavings of Parmesan cheese on top.

Chinese Chow Mein

SERVES 2

Practise this recipe and you'll dispense with the need to run out to your local Chinese takeaway just before the film begins on TV.

175g (6oz) medium egg noodles
1 large garlic clove
1 small mild red chilli
2.5cm (1in) piece of fresh root ginger
175g (6oz) cooked turkey
4 spring onions
50g (2oz) button mushrooms
1 small red pepper
2 tablespoons sunflower oil
50g (2oz) bean sprouts
1–2 teaspoons sesame oil
2 tablespoons dark soy sauce

① Break the noodles into a large pan of boiling water and leave to cook for 2 minutes.

② Finely slice the garlic. Cut the chilli in half, scoop out the seeds with a teaspoon and cut into thin slices. Put the garlic and chilli in a small bowl.

③ Drain the noodles and rinse under cold running water, then drain again thoroughly. Set aside.

④ Peel and finely chop the ginger. Add to the garlic mixture.

⑤ Cut the turkey into thin strips. Cut the spring onions into 2cm (¾in) lengths. Thinly slice the mushrooms. Cut the pepper in half, remove the core and seeds and thinly slice the flesh.

⑥ Heat a wok or large frying pan. Add the sunflower oil then the garlic mixture. Stir-fry for about 30 seconds. Add the turkey, spring onions, mushrooms and pepper and stir-fry for another 1–2 minutes. Add the bean sprouts and toss to combine.

❼ Add the noodles, sesame oil and soy sauce and toss well to coat, then cook for another 2–3 minutes, without stirring, until the noodles are beginning to crisp underneath.

❽ Turn the noodles out on to warmed serving plates and serve at once.

Sesame Turkey and Garlic Fried Rice

SERVES 2-3

This recipe uses pre-cooked rice. If you prepare it on a previous day, do make sure that it is cooked thoroughly and then refrigerate it.

300g (10oz) turkey escalopes
4 tablespoons dark soy sauce
2 tablespoons dry sherry
2 teaspoons sesame oil
1 tablespoon sesame seeds
2 teaspoons cornflour
175g (6oz) broccoli
100g (4oz) baby sweetcorn
5cm (2in) piece of fresh root ginger
4 tablespoons groundnut oil
1 medium onion
4 large garlic cloves
1–2 teaspoons sugar
120ml (4fl oz) chicken stock
300g (10oz) cold cooked long-grain rice
1 teaspoon arrowroot
a small bunch of fresh coriander
salt and freshly ground black pepper
2 red chilli flowers, to garnish (see page 49)

❶ Cut the turkey diagonally into strips and put in a bowl. Add 1 tablespoon of the soy sauce, 1 tablespoon of the sherry, 1 teaspoon of the sesame oil, the sesame seeds, cornflour, salt and pepper and mix well together.

❷ Cut the broccoli into small florets and the sweetcorn diagonally in half. Put in a saucepan of boiling salted water and blanch for 2 minutes, then drain and refresh under cold running water.

❸ Heat a wok or large frying pan. Cut the ginger into thin slices and then finely chop. Add half the groundnut and the remaining sesame oil to the wok, add the ginger and stir-fry for 1 minute until crispy. Add the turkey mixture and stir-fry for 5 minutes or until lightly browned.

❹ In another wok, heat the remaining groundnut oil. Roughly chop the onion and garlic and add to the oil. Season with salt and pepper and stir-fry for 3–4 minutes.

5 Add the remaining soy sauce, the sugar and stock to the turkey and simmer gently for 6–8 minutes until the sauce has reduced.

6 Add the rice to the onion mixture, season and cook for 4–5 minutes.

7 Blend the arrowroot with the remaining sherry. Add to the turkey with the broccoli and sweetcorn and stir-fry for 1–2 minutes.

8 Chop the coriander and stir into the rice. Pile into warmed serving bowls, spoon the turkey over the rice and serve garnished with the chilli flowers.

Chilli flowers *To make chilli flowers, wear rubber gloves and hold a small red chilli by its stem. Using a small pair of scissors, cut around the chilli to form petals, taking care not to cut all the way to the stem. Remove the seeds. Plunge the cut chillies into a bowl of cold water and store in the fridge until they open out to form flowers.*

Coronation Turkey

SERVES 2

This is great to serve on a hot summer's day along with some barbecued foods or – my favourite way of eating it – inside a warm baguette!

175g (6oz) long-grain and wild rice mix
1 small onion
40g (1½oz) butter
8 ready-to-eat apricots
2 tablespoons korma curry paste
1 tablespoon clear honey
a good splash of dry white wine
225g (8oz) asparagus spears
4 spring onions
2 tablespoons sunflower oil
1 tablespoon fresh lemon juice
½ teaspoon chilli sauce
2 teaspoons tiny dill sprigs, plus sprigs to garnish
300g (10oz) cooked turkey
6 tablespoons mayonnaise
3 tablespoons double cream
salt and freshly ground black pepper

1 Put the rice in a saucepan with plenty of boiling salted water, cover and simmer for 10–15 minutes until tender.

2 Finely chop the onion. Melt the butter in a small pan, add the onion and fry for 3–5 minutes until softened. Using scissors, finely chop the apricots. Add to the onion with the curry paste, 2 teaspoons of the honey, the wine, salt and pepper and simmer for about 5 minutes until well reduced and syrupy.

3 Meanwhile, trim the asparagus then cut into 4cm (1½in) lengths. Plunge into a small pan of boiling salted water and cook for 2 minutes until just tender. Trim the spring onions, cut into 2cm (¾in) lengths and add to the pan. Tip into a colander and rinse well under cold water.

49

4 Tip the fried onion mixture into a bowl and set aside to cool a little.

5 In a screw-topped jar, shake together the remaining honey, the oil, lemon juice, chilli sauce, dill sprigs, salt and pepper until well mixed.

6 Remove any skin from the turkey and cut into bite-sized pieces. Drain off any excess oil from the fried onion mixture, then stir in the mayonnaise and cream. Carefully fold in the turkey.

7 Drain the rice and rinse well under cold running water. Put in a bowl and add the dressing and vegetables. Toss together until well mixed.

8 Arrange the rice around serving plates and pile the turkey mixture in the middle. Garnish with dill sprigs and serve at once.

Marmalade Duck with Celeriac Purée

SERVES 2

Ideally, duck should be served slightly undercooked so that it remains tender and full flavoured, but the fact always remains that you should cook your meat the way you like it.

two 150g (5oz) duck breasts, well trimmed
350g (12oz) potatoes
225g (8oz) celeriac
sunflower oil, for frying
1 carrot
1 small leek
2 heaped tablespoons bitter orange marmalade
150ml (¼ pint) dry white wine
150ml (¼ pint) fresh chicken stock
75g (3oz) unsalted butter
1 tablespoon chopped fresh parsley
50–75ml (2–3fl oz) milk
salt and freshly ground black pepper

1 Heat a heavy-based frying pan. Score the duck, skin-side up, in a lattice pattern and season well with salt and pepper. Add to the pan, skin-side down, and cook for 10–12 minutes if you like it medium done, turning occasionally.

2 Meanwhile, peel and cube the potatoes. Peel and cube the celeriac into slightly smaller pieces than the potato. Put both in a saucepan of boiling salted water, cover and cook for about 10 minutes or until tender.

3 Heat about 2.5cm (1in) of the oil in a wok or deep frying pan. Using a vegetable peeler, peel the carrot and slice it into ribbons. Stack up the ribbons and then slice

lengthways into fine strips. Shred the leek. Add the carrot and leek to the wok and deep-fry for 2–3 minutes until the oil stops bubbling. Drain on kitchen paper and leave to crisp up.

4 In a pan, warm the marmalade with a splash of wine then sieve to remove the peel.

5 Remove the duck from the pan and leave to rest in a warm place. Drain off any excess fat from the pan, pour in the remaining wine and bring to the boil, stirring to remove any sediment from the bottom. Add the stock and sieved marmalade and boil rapidly for about 5 minutes.

6 Drain the celeriac and potatoes, mash with a potato masher then season with plenty of pepper. Beat in 25g (1oz) of the butter, the parsley and enough milk to make a smooth purée.

7 Dice the remaining butter, then whisk a piece at a time into the sauce.

8 Spoon the purée on to warmed serving plates. Carve the duck diagonally into slices and fan out on top of the purée. Drizzle over some of the sauce and garnish with the crispy vegetables. Serve at once.

VEGET
DISHES

Spring Vegetable Baskets

SERVES 2

The great thing about filo pastry is that it's so easy to use. The important point to remember is that it dries out very quickly so it must be kept covered with a damp tea-towel prior to baking.

| 175g (6oz) butter |
| 8 sheets of filo pastry, thawed if frozen |
| 2 egg yolks |
| a pinch of salt |
| 1 teaspoon hot water |
| 1 tablespoon mild olive oil |
| 225g (8oz) mixed spring vegetables, such as asparagus tips, baby carrots, sweetcorn and mange-tout peas |
| 1 tablespoon chopped fresh tarragon |
| juice of 1 lemon |

1 Pre-heat the oven to 200°C/400°F/Gas 6.

2 Melt the butter in a small saucepan. Cut the filo pastry into eight 17.5cm (7in) squares. Put two 150ml (¼ pint) glass ramekin dishes, upturned, on a baking tray and brush with butter. Layer 4 pastry squares on top, brushing each liberally with the melted butter, to make 2 baskets.

3 Bake the baskets for 8–10 minutes until crisp and golden. Remove from the oven and carefully lift each basket off its ramekin and place on a wire rack to cool completely.

4 Meanwhile, in a heatproof bowl, whisk the egg yolks with the hot water and a pinch of salt until well combined. Stand the bowl over a pan of gently simmering water and whisk for 2–3 minutes until the mixture is thick enough to leave a trail.

5 Heat a small wok or frying pan with a little of the melted butter and the oil. Cut in half lengthways any of the vegetables that are particularly thick. Add the vegetables to the wok and stir-fry for about 1 minute. Sprinkle in 2–3 tablespoons water and

continue to steam-fry the vegetables for 2–3 minutes until tender.

6 Meanwhile, make the sauce. Gradually pour the melted butter into the egg mixture a little at a time, whisking constantly. Stir in 2 teaspoons of the tarragon and enough lemon juice to achieve a creamy consistency. Keep warm.

7 Spoon some of the sauce into the middle of warmed serving plates, place one of the pastry cases in the middle of each and fill with some of the vegetables and a little of the sauce. Garnish with the remaining tarragon and serve at once.

Mozzarella and Spinach Ravioli

SERVES 2

It is surprisingly easy to make fresh pasta, and the combination of spinach and mozzarella is lovely when used as a filling in the ravioli.

165g (5½oz) plain flour, plus extra for dusting
2 eggs, plus beaten egg for sealing
3 tablespoons olive oil
1 tablespoon lukewarm water
dry semolina, for dusting
225g (8oz) tender young spinach leaves
a knob of butter
100g (4oz) mozzarella cheese
2 tablespoons freshly grated Parmesan cheese, plus shavings to garnish
a little freshly grated nutmeg
1 shallot
1 garlic clove
150ml (¼ pint) passata (see page 55)
2 tablespoons chopped fresh mixed herbs, such as chives, parsley and oregano
2 tablespoons toasted pine kernels
salt and freshly ground black pepper

1 Put the flour in a food processor and, with the motor running, add the 2 eggs, 1 tablespoon of the olive oil and the water. Whizz for 1 minute. Turn out on to a lightly floured work surface and knead lightly to a smooth dough.

2 Divide the dough into 3 pieces and roll out each piece into a very thin rectangle, dusting with a little semolina if necessary to prevent sticking.

3 Wash the spinach and put it in a saucepan with only the water clinging to the leaves after washing. Add the butter and cook until wilted down. Meanwhile, dice the mozzarella cheese. Drain the spinach, leave to cool a little then squeeze dry. Roughly chop and place in a bowl with the mozzarella cheese, Parmesan cheese, nutmeg, salt and pepper. Mix well.

4 Brush the pasta sheets with the beaten egg and place 2 heaped tablespoons of the mozzarella mixture on one half of each. Flip over the other half of the rectangle to cover the filling completely. Press down around the filling to enclose and then, using a sharp knife, cut out the pasta into 10cm (4in) squares. Dust with a little more semolina.

❺ Heat a large deep frying pan with about 4cm (1½in) water. Carefully add the ravioli (in batches, if necessary) and poach for about 5 minutes or until tender.

❻ Meanwhile, finely chop the shallot. Crush the garlic. Heat the remaining 2 tablespoons of oil in a frying pan. Add the shallot and stir-fry for 1–2 minutes. Stir

in the garlic and cook for a further 30 seconds. Pour the passata into the shallot mixture and season with salt and pepper to taste. Simmer for 1–2 minutes then stir in the herbs and pine kernels.

❼ Drain the pasta, return to the pan and pour in the tomato sauce, stirring to coat. Spoon the pasta into warmed, wide rimmed bowls, scatter with some Parmesan shavings and serve at once.

....

Passata is sieved tomatoes and can be found in jars and cartons.

Tomato and Spinach Risotto

SERVES 2

....

The finished risotto should be rich and creamy. This is achieved by adding stock a little at a time and allowing it to be absorbed into the rice.

1 garlic clove
1 small onion
2 tablespoons olive oil
400g (14oz) can chopped tomatoes
600ml (1 pint) vegetable stock
150g (5oz) risotto rice
225g (8oz) spinach leaves
15g (½oz) unsalted butter
4–6 sun-dried tomatoes, preserved in oil
25g (1oz) block of Parmesan cheese
salt and freshly ground black pepper

❶ Crush the garlic and finely chop the onion. Heat the oil in a frying pan, add the garlic and onion and fry for 2–3 minutes until softened.

❷ Pour the tomatoes and stock into a small saucepan, bring to the boil, then reduce the heat to a gentle simmer.

❸ Stir the rice into the frying pan with the onion and garlic and stir-fry until well coated. Add 1 ladleful of the stock mixture, stirring until absorbed, then add another ladle of stock and continue until nearly all the stock has been used. This will take about 15 minutes. Season with salt and pepper to taste.

❹ Meanwhile, wash the spinach and put it in a pan, with only the water still clinging to the leaves after washing, a knob of the butter and salt and pepper, and cook for 2–3 minutes until just tender. Tip into a bowl and leave to cool a little.

5 Snip the sun-dried tomatoes into small dice. Shave off some slices of the Parmesan cheese, set aside for garnish, then grate the remainder.

6 Squeeze out the excess moisture from the spinach and roughly chop.

7 Just after adding the last ladleful of stock to the rice, stir in the diced tomatoes, grated cheese, remaining butter and the spinach and cook until all the liquid has been absorbed and the rice is just tender.

8 Spoon the risotto into bowls, garnish with the Parmesan shavings and serve.

Italian Filo Vegetable Tarts

SERVES 2

By brushing each layer of pastry with melted butter, you will achieve a light and crispy finish

25g (1oz) butter
six 12.5cm (5in) squares of filo pastry
1 small red onion
2 tablespoons olive oil
2 large chestnut mushrooms
a small handful of fresh parsley
1 garlic clove
2 teaspoons lemon juice
3 sun-dried tomatoes preserved in oil
100g (4oz) mozzarella cheese
4 small tomatoes
2 pitted black olives
a few fresh basil leaves
a little freshly grated Parmesan cheese
a few pretty salad leaves, ideally rocket
salt and freshly ground black pepper

1 Pre-heat the oven to 200°C/400°F/Gas 6.

2 Melt the butter. Brush 2 individual 9cm (3½ in) tartlet tins with butter then brush the sheets of filo with butter. Layer 3 sheets into each of the tins, overlapping the pastry to form a star shape, with corners of filo pastry sticking out from the tins like petals. Place on a baking tray and bake for 6–7 minutes until golden.

3 Very thinly slice the onion. Heat a frying pan and add 1 tablespoon of the oil. Add the onion to the pan and fry. Meanwhile, finely chop the mushrooms then add to the onion. Chop the parsley and crush the garlic. Add to the pan with the lemon juice and season with salt and pepper. Roughly chop the sun-dried tomatoes, add to the pan, then check the seasoning.

4 Remove the tarts from the oven and fill each tart with half the vegetable mixture.

5 Cut half of the mozzarella cheese into cubes and scatter on top of the tarts. Cut 2 slices from a tomato and add one to each tart. Cut the olives in half and arrange the halves on the tomato slices with a basil leaf.

6 Sprinkle with a little Parmesan cheese and return to the oven for 2–3 minutes to warm the mozzarella cheese.

7 Meanwhile, slice the remaining tomatoes and mozzarella cheese and arrange around the edge of serving plates. Place a few salad and basil leaves on top.

Drizzle over the remaining oil and season with salt and pepper.

8 Remove the tarts from the oven, carefully lift them out of the tins and place in the centre of the salads to serve.

Cheddar Cheese Patties with Mustard Seed Relish

SERVES 2

This lovely vegetarian dish is perfect as a luncheon snack, served with a tomato and basil salad.

1 small carrot
1 small parsnip
1 courgette
1 tablespoon mustard seeds
4 tablespoons sunflower oil
1 large shallot
225g (8fl oz) cider vinegar
25g (1oz) caster sugar
1 red-skinned apple
grated rind and juice of ½ a lemon
75g (3oz) mature Cheddar cheese
100g (4oz) fresh white breadcrumbs
1 spring onion
2 small eggs
3 tablespoons chopped fresh parsley
a pinch of English mustard powder
a pinch of freshly grated nutmeg
¼ teaspoon dried thyme
plain flour, to dust
15g (½oz) butter

1 Using a vegetable peeler, peel the carrot and parsnip then shred the carrot, parsnip and courgette into ribbons, into a bowl of iced cold water. Put the mustard seeds in a small bowl of warm water and leave to soak for 30 minutes then drain.

2 Heat 2 tablespoons of the oil in a small saucepan, add the shallot and fry for 2–3 minutes until softened. Add the soaked mustard seeds, cider vinegar and sugar and boil until reduced to a third. Finely chop the apple, add to the pan with the lemon rind and cook for a further 4–5 minutes.

3 Meanwhile, grate the cheese and put in a bowl with 75g (3oz) of the breadcrumbs. Finely chop the spring onion and add to the bowl with one of the eggs, 2 tablespoons of the parsley, mustard powder, nutmeg and thyme. Mix well, squeezing the mixture together with your hands.

4 Beat the remaining egg. Shape the mixture into 4 patties then roll in the flour, the egg and the remaining 25g (1oz) of breadcrumbs. Mark the patties with a palette knife, by gently pressing the knife on top.

❺ Heat 1 tablespoon of the oil and the butter in a frying pan. When foaming, add the patties and fry for 2–3 minutes on each side, until golden.

❻ Drain the curled-up vegetables on to a tea-towel and pat dry. Heat the remaining oil in a wok or frying pan. Add the vegetables to the wok with the lemon juice and remaining 1 tablespoon of parsley and stir-fry for 2–3 minutes. To serve, spoon the vegetable ribbons on to warmed serving plates then add the cheese patties and a spoonful of the relish.

Vegetable Lasagne

SERVES 2

It's worth spending a little more and buying fresh, rather than dried, lasagne. It's nicer to handle, easier to cook and tastes better.

150ml (¼ pint) vegetable stock
150ml (¼ pint) dry white wine
4 sheets of fresh lasagne
50ml (2fl oz) double cream
1 small carrot
4 spring onions
100g (4oz) fine green beans
1 small courgette
50g (2oz) unsalted butter
1 tablespoon light olive oil
¼ teaspoon cayenne
1 teaspoon light soy sauce
a squeeze of lime juice
2 tablespoons chopped fresh coriander
2oz (50g) freshly grated Pecorino or Parmesan cheese

❶ Put the vegetable stock and wine in a small saucepan and simmer until well reduced and slightly syrupy.

❷ Meanwhile, using scissors, cut the lasagne sheets into 10 x 10cm (4 x 4in) squares.

❸ Whip the cream until it just holds its shape then set aside.

❹ Using a vegetable peeler, peel the carrot then shred long thin ribbons down its length. Cut the spring onions and fine green beans into 5cm (2in) lengths. Cut the courgette into batons, 5cm (2in) long and 1cm (½in) thick.

❺ Plunge the lasagne squares into a large saucepan of boiling salted water and cook for 2 minutes until just tender. Remove with a slotted spoon and drain on kitchen paper. Heat a knob of butter and the oil in a wok or large frying pan and stir-fry the green beans and courgette for 1–2 minutes. Add a little of the reducing stock, the spring onions and carrot and continue to steam-fry for a further 1–2 minutes. Add the cayenne, soy sauce and lime juice. Remove from the heat.

❻ Whisk the remaining butter into the

reduced stock mixture then mix in the coriander. Add the cream and whisk again.

7 Pre-heat the grill. Arrange a square of lasagne in each of 2 warmed flameproof bowls and spoon over some of the vegetables. Cover with another square of lasagne and add the remaining vegetables. Spoon over the sauce. Sprinkle with the cheese.

8 Place the bowls under the grill until the cheese is golden brown. Serve at once.

Florentine Puffs with Mixed Bean Salad

SERVES 2

With such a wide range of interesting beans available in health shops and supermarkets its never been easier to create stunning salads.
So go on, be creative!

225g (8oz) spinach
225g (8oz) puff pastry (ready-rolled is ideal)
50g (2oz) mature Cheddar cheese
a pinch of freshly grated nutmeg
1 egg, beaten
1 teaspoon sesame seeds
100g (4oz) green beans
¼ cucumber
2 spring onions
200g (7oz) can red kidney beans, drained
200g (7oz) can butter beans, drained
3 tablespoons olive oil
1 tablespoon red wine vinegar
1 teaspoon wholegrain mustard
a pinch of caster sugar
a small handful of fresh chives
100g (4oz) cherry tomatoes
salt and freshly ground black pepper

1 Pre-heat the oven to 220°C/425°F/Gas 7.

2 Wash the spinach, remove the stalks and put in a saucepan with just the water that clings to the leaves. Cover and cook for 3 minutes, shaking the pan frequently.

3 On a lightly floured surface, if necessary, roll out the pastry and cut into two 15cm (6in) squares.

4 Drain the spinach and squeeze out the excess water. Put the spinach on a chopping board, roughly chop and put in a bowl. Grate the cheese. Add to the spinach with the nutmeg, salt and pepper and mix together.

5 Pile the spinach mixture in the centre of the pastry squares. Brush the edges of the pastry with beaten egg. Fold the corners of the pastry to the middle and press the edges together to seal, leaving the centre open. Fold back the corners about 2.5cm (1in) to show the filling. Brush with beaten egg and sprinkle with the sesame seeds.

⑥ Put the puffs on a baking tray and bake in the oven for 10 minutes until golden brown.

⑦ Meanwhile, cut the green beans into 2.5cm (1in) lengths. Cook in a pan of boiling water for 3 minutes. Dice the cucumber. Diagonally slice the spring onions. Drain the green beans and refresh under cold running water. Put the green beans, cucumber, spring onions, kidney and butter beans in a bowl.

⑧ Whisk together the oil, vinegar, mustard, sugar, salt and pepper. Pour two-thirds of the dressing over the bean salad and toss together. Snip the chives and mix into the remaining salad dressing.

⑨ Cut the cherry tomatoes in half. Put the florentine puffs on serving plates. Pile the cherry tomatoes on the plates and drizzle over the chive dressing. Serve with the mixed bean salad.

Tomato Soup with Cheesy Soda Bread

SERVES 2

This is the perfect recipe for children to make. The only stage that needs extra supervision is the blending process, and the cleaning up afterwards!

FOR THE SOUP
6 plum tomatoes, weighing about 450g (1lb)
1 large potato, weighing about 250g (9oz)
1 shallot
2 large garlic cloves
2 tablespoons olive oil, plus about 75ml (3fl oz)
600ml (1 pint) hot vegetable stock
1 large basil plant
a pinch of caster sugar
4 tablespoons soured cream
salt and freshly ground black pepper
FOR THE BREAD
6 fresh sage leaves

75g (3oz) Gruyère cheese
350g (12oz) plain flour
1 teaspoon salt
1 teaspoon bicarbonate of soda
1 teaspoon baking powder
1 teaspoon mustard powder
300ml (½ pint) buttermilk

❶ To make the bread, finely chop the sage. Grate the Gruyère cheese. Sift the flour into a bowl then stir in the salt, bicarbonate of soda, baking powder, mustard powder, cheese and sage. Add the buttermilk and mix, with a round-bladed knife, to form a soft dough.

❷ Heat a griddle pan or heavy-based frying

pan. On a heavily floured surface, pat the dough into a round flat disc about 2.5cm (1in) thick. Cut the disc into 4 triangles. Cook on the griddle pan for 15 minutes, turning occasionally, until well risen and golden brown.

❸ To make the soup, roughly chop the tomatoes and put in a bowl. Peel the potato and cut into small dice. Roughly chop the shallot and garlic. Heat the 2 tablespoons of olive oil in a large saucepan, add the shallot and half of the garlic and cook for 3–4 minutes until softened. Add the chopped tomatoes, diced potato and vegetable stock. Strip a handful of leaves from the basil plant. Add to the pan, bring to the boil, cover and simmer for 8 minutes until the potato is tender.

❹ Strip the remaining leaves off the basil plant and put in a food processor with the remaining garlic and a little of the remaining oil. Whiz for 2–3 seconds then pour in enough oil to make a smooth, thick purée. Pour into a small jug.

❺ Using a hand blender, purée the soup. Add salt, pepper and sugar to taste.

❻ Ladle the soup into warmed bowls, put a spoonful of the soured cream in the centre and then swirl in some of the basil purée. Serve with the warm cheesy soda bread.

Mixed Mushroom Risotto with Wilted Greens

SERVES 2

There's no excuse for using 'boring' mushrooms with every supermarket now stocking a wide selection of fresh and dried – so go wild with your selection.

15g (½oz) dried cep or porcini mushrooms (optional)	cheese, plus shavings to serve
300ml (½ pint) boiling water	4 tablespoons chopped fresh flat-leaved parsley
600ml (1 pint) vegetable stock	salt and freshly ground black pepper
1 shallot	FOR THE WILTED GREENS
2 garlic cloves	3 tablespoons olive oil
2 tablespoons olive oil	2 garlic cloves
225g (8oz) risotto rice	1 small red chilli
250g (9oz) firm mixed mushrooms, such as flat, chestnut and button	juice of ½ a lemon
50g (2oz) butter	75g (3oz) mixed baby leaves, such as lambs lettuce, rocket and watercress
2 tablespoons freshly grated Parmesan	sea salt

❶ If using, put the dried mushrooms in a bowl and pour the boiling water over them. Leave to soak.

❷ Pour the stock into a saucepan, bring to the boil, then reduce the heat to a gentle simmer.

❸ Finely chop the shallot and garlic. Heat 1 tablespoon of the olive oil in a large saucepan, add the shallot and garlic and fry for 3–4 minutes until softened. Add the rice and cook for a further 1 minute.

❹ Keeping the heat fairly high, add a ladleful of hot stock to the rice and stir until it has been absorbed. Continue to gradually stir in the stock over a gentle heat until it has all been absorbed. This will take about 15 minutes.

❺ Meanwhile, prepare the dressing for the wilted greens. Pour the olive oil into a small pan and heat gently. Peel and halve the garlic. Halve the chilli and remove the seeds. Add the garlic and chilli to the oil and heat very gently for 10 minutes until the garlic has softened but barely coloured.

❻ Meanwhile, remove the soaked mushrooms from the liquid and add to the risotto. Stir the soaking liquid into the stock and continue to add to the risotto.

❼ Slice the fresh mushrooms. Heat the remaining 1 tablespoon of oil and a knob of the butter in a frying pan, add the mushrooms and cook over a high heat for 3–4 minutes. Stir the fried mushrooms, grated Parmesan cheese and remaining butter into the risotto. Add the parsley and salt and pepper to taste. Remove from the heat and cover.

❽ Remove the garlic and chilli from the oil and discard. Stir the lemon juice and plenty of black pepper into the oil and heat gently. Pour the dressing over the baby leaves and toss well together. Sprinkle with sea salt.

❾ Spoon the risotto into warmed serving bowls and pile the wilted greens in the centre. Scatter shavings of Parmesan on top of the greens and serve at once.

FISH
DISHES

Pan-Fried Salmon and Watercress Sauce

SERVES 2

This recipe calls for fish stock and, while it's not difficult to make, it does require a little more effort. However, help is at hand. All good supermarkets stock fresh fish stock in cartons. So no need to worry!

about 1 tablespoon light olive oil
300g (10oz) baby new potatoes
1 carrot
1 courgette
40g (1½oz) unsalted butter
2 salmon fillets, each weighing about 150g (5oz)
150ml (¼ pint) dry white wine
25g (1oz) watercress, plus extra to garnish
75ml (3fl oz) fish stock (see below)
120ml (4fl oz) crème fraiche
salt and freshly ground black pepper

Fish stock *Look for fish stock in cartons in your supermarket, it is far superior to stock cubes.*

❶ Pre-heat the oven to 180C/350F/Gas 4. Line 2 ramekin dishes with clingfilm and brush with oil.

❷ Cut the potatoes in half, put in a saucepan of cold salted water and bring to the boil. Cover and cook for 10–12 minutes until tender.

❸ Bring a small pan of water to the boil. Peel the carrot and cut it and the courgette into matchstick-sized strips. Add the carrot to the pan and cook for 1 minute, then add the courgette and cook for a further 30 seconds. Drain the vegetables and refresh under cold running water. Dry on kitchen paper and put in a small bowl.

❹ Melt a knob of the butter in the same pan and add to the vegetables. Season well with salt and pepper. Put the vegetables in the prepared ramekin dishes and flatten down with a palette knife. Place in the oven for 6–8 minutes to heat through.

❺ Meanwhile, heat a little oil and a knob of butter in a frying pan. Season the salmon fillets and add to the pan. Cook for 2 minutes on each side until just tender and lightly golden. Remove from the pan, cover with foil and set aside. Add the wine to the pan and boil to reduce down to about 1 tablespoon.

❻ Put the watercress and stock in a food processor and whiz until blended. Pour into the pan with the crème fraiche. Season and cook for 2–3 minutes until reduced, stirring occasionally. Return the salmon to the pan and cook until just heated through.

7 Meanwhile, drain the potatoes and toss in the remaining butter. Turn the vegetables out of the ramekin dishes.

8 Arrange the salmon fillets on warmed serving plates and spoon some of the sauce around them. Add the potatoes and a vegetable mound. Garnish with a sprig of watercress and serve at once.

Prawn Cocktail

SERVES 2

This classic starter is an ideal dish to serve as a first course for a dinner party or as a snack for you and your friends and family. It is the epitome of good food without having to work hard to make it.

3 tablespoons mayonnaise
2 tablespoons double cream
1 teaspoon tomato purée
a dash of Worcestershire sauce
1 small lemon
175g (6oz) cooked peeled prawns
2 iceberg lettuce leaves
butter, for spreading
2 slices of brown soda bread
salt and freshly ground black pepper

1 In a small bowl, mix together the mayonnaise, cream, tomato purée and Worcestershire sauce. Add a squeeze of lemon juice and season with salt and pepper to taste. Add the prawns and stir well to coat.

2 Arrange the lettuce leaves on top of each other and shred into 5mm (¼ in) ribbons. Place in the bottom of glass serving dishes, top with the prawn mixture and garnish with slices of the lemon.

3 Butter the bread and cut the slices in half. Stand the prawn cocktails on small plates and serve the bread on the side.

Trout and Parma Ham Rolls

SERVES 2

This might appear to be an unusual marriage of ingredients but, believe me, the flavour combination is fabulous.

25g (1oz) pine kernels
3 sun-dried tomatoes
a small bunch of flat-leaved parsley
300g (10oz) cooked basmati rice (about 120g/4½oz uncooked)
2 heaped tablespoons raisins
about 4 tablespoons olive oil
about 40g (1½oz) unsalted butter
4 small trout fillets, each weighing about 100g (4oz)
4 large slices of Parma ham
6 sage leaves
150ml (¼ pint) dry white wine
25g (1oz) tender young spinach leaves
25g (1oz) watercress
1 lemon
salt and freshly ground black pepper

1 Pre-heat the oven to 200°C/400°F/Gas 6.

2 Put the pine kernels in a small frying pan and dry-fry for a few minutes until toasted. Finely chop the sun-dried tomatoes and parsley.

3 Put the rice in a bowl with the pine kernels, raisins, sun-dried tomatoes, parsley and a little oil to moisten. Season generously with salt and pepper.

4 Pack into 2 well buttered ring (12.5cm/5in) moulds. Level the tops and place on a baking tray. Bake for 6–8 minutes until heated through.

5 Heat a knob of the butter and a little of the oil in a frying pan. Smear the trout with some of the butter and season with pepper. Lay the Parma ham on the work surface and place a sage leaf in the middle of each slice. Top with the trout, buttered-side down, and roll up. Secure with cocktail sticks. Add the trout to the pan and cook over a high heat for 2–3 minutes on each side until lightly golden.

6 Pour in the wine and allow some to evaporate, then reduce the heat and cook for a further 6–8 minutes until the fish is tender and cooked through and you have a well-flavoured sauce.

7 Remove the moulds from the oven. Place an inverted serving plate on top of each mould then turn over to turn out. Leave to cool a little.

8 Wash the spinach and put in a bowl with the watercress. Season and add a little oil and a squeeze of lemon. Toss to coat.

9 Shred the remaining sage leaves and add to the fish. Squeeze over the remaining lemon juice and then remove from the heat.

10 Arrange the spinach salad in the centre of the rice rings and place 2 trout on top of each. Spoon the sauce around them and serve at once.

Peppered Cod Steaks with Ratatouille

SERVES 2

I really love this dish. It's a flavour-pack of sunshine ingredients and always reminds me of holidays in the south of France. Oh, and by the way, it's ever so easy to make!

25g (1oz) unsalted butter
4 thin slices of white bread
1 shallot
2 baby aubergines or 75g (3oz) piece of aubergine
1 small courgette
½ small red pepper
2 tomatoes
4 tablespoons olive oil
2 tablespoons sun-dried tomato purée
1 heaped tablespoon mixed peppercorns
1 tablespoon plain flour
two 200g (7oz) fresh cod fillets
1 garlic clove
a small bunch of flat-leaved parsley
1 small lemon
salt and freshly ground black pepper

❶ Pre-heat the oven to 200C/400F/Gas 6.

❷ Melt the butter. Cut off the crusts from the bread and brush both sides with the butter. Press firmly into two 9cm (3½in) tartlet tins. Place on a baking tray and bake in the oven for 10–12 minutes until crisp and golden.

❸ Finely chop the shallot. Dice the aubergine and courgette. Remove the core and seeds from the pepper and dice the flesh. Chop the tomatoes, discarding the seeds.

❹ Heat 3 tablespoons of the oil in a frying pan. Add the shallot and cook for 2–3 minutes until softened. Add the aubergine, courgette and pepper, stirring to coat in the oil. Add the tomatoes and tomato purée and cook for 8–10 minutes, stirring occasionally. Season with salt and pepper to taste.

❺ In a pestle and mortar, crush the peppercorns. Put on a plate with the flour, season with a pinch of salt and mix well. Remove the skin from the fish and wipe the fish with kitchen paper. Coat in the peppercorn mixture, pressing well on both sides.

❻ Heat the remaining oil in a frying pan. Add the fish and fry for 2–3 minutes on each side, until crisp and golden.

❼ Meanwhile, make the gremolata. Finely chop the garlic and parsley. Grate the lemon rind and put in a small bowl with the garlic mixture. Mix well together.

❽ Remove the bread baskets from the oven and place on warmed serving plates. Spoon in the ratatouille and arrange the fish at the side. Sprinkle with the gremolata and serve at once.

Thai Fish Kebabs with Crispy Mango Salad

SERVES 2

This recipe calls for tuna steaks but if you are unable to get fresh tuna, or find it too meaty for your liking, try halibut or whiting.

1 tuna steak, weighing about 150g (5oz)
4 plaice fillets, each weighing about 100g (4oz)
8 raw tiger prawns
1 garlic clove
1 teaspoon grated fresh root ginger
grated rind and juice of 2 limes
2 tablespoons chopped fresh coriander
2 teaspoons sesame oil
1 small mango
1 small carrot
50g (2oz) mange-tout peas
a handful of radicchio leaves
2 spring onions
50g (2oz) bean sprouts
salt and freshly ground black pepper
2 radish flowers, to garnish (see below)

❶ Pre-heat the grill and cover the grill pan with a piece of kitchen foil. Soak 4 wooden skewers.

❷ Cut the tuna steak into 8 even-sized cubes. Cut each plaice fillet in half lengthways to make 8 thin strips. Roll up and thread alternately on to the skewers with the tuna cubes and the prawns.

❸ Crush the garlic and put in a bowl. Add the ginger, lime rind and juice, coriander and sesame oil and mix well together. Season with salt and pepper to taste and pour half into a shallow flameproof dish. Add the skewers and turn to coat. Set aside.

❹ Peel the mango and cut the flesh into thin slices, then into matchsticks. Place in a large bowl.

❺ Place the kebabs on the grill pan and grill for about 8 minutes until cooked through, turning occasionally.

❻ Meanwhile, peel the carrot and cut it into matchsticks and cut the mange-tout into thin strips. Shred the radicchio leaves and slice the spring onions. Add them to the mango with the bean sprouts.

❼ Place a 7.5cm (3in) plain cutter in the middle of warmed serving plates and pack in the salad mixture. Remove the ring, arrange the fish kebabs around the salad and garnish with the radish flowers. Serve at once.

Radish Flowers To make a radish flower, use a small knife and make 5 cuts around the radish, almost to the stalk end. Put into a bowl of iced water and leave until the petals open out.

Tuna and Cheese Soufflés

SERVES 2–4

This is such a nice recipe and ever so easy to follow. It's also fail-safe, providing you make sure that the egg whites are really well whisked and you take care when folding them into the cheese mixture.

50g (2oz) butter, plus extra for greasing
2 tablespoons freshly grated Parmesan cheese
1 tablespoon plain flour
1 teaspoon Dijon mustard
a little paprika
100ml (3½fl oz) milk
50g (2oz) mature Cheddar cheese
2 eggs
100g (4oz) can tuna in brine, drained
two 225g (8oz) baking potatoes
a small bunch of watercress
salt and freshly ground black pepper

❶ Pre-heat the oven to 220°C/400°F/Gas 6. Grease four 100ml (4fl oz) ramekin dishes with butter and sprinkle some of the Parmesan cheese into each one, tilting until evenly coated.

❷ Melt 15g (½oz) of the butter in a small saucepan and stir in the flour and mustard. Season with salt and pepper, add a little paprika and cook for 1 minute, stirring.

❸ Remove from the heat and gradually stir in the milk until smooth. Slowly bring to the boil and cook, stirring, until thickened. Leave to cool.

❹ Meanwhile, grate the Cheddar cheese.

Separate the eggs and whisk the egg whites until they stand in soft peaks. Stir half the cheese into the sauce then stir in the egg yolks, one at a time. Add the tuna and mix well. Mix one large spoonful of the egg whites into the sauce to lighten it, then fold in the rest until just combined – do not over-mix.

❺ Pour the soufflé mixture into the prepared dishes and sprinkle with the remaining Cheddar cheese. Arrange on a baking tray and run a knife around the top edge of each dish. Bake for about 10–12 minutes until well risen and golden.

❻ Meanwhile, peel the potatoes and cut each into 8 wedges. Put in a saucepan of cold salted water, cover, bring to the boil and cook for 5–6 minutes until just tender.

❼ Pre-heat the grill and cover the grill pan with a piece of kitchen foil.

❽ Melt the remaining butter in a pan and add a little more paprika. Drain the potatoes and refresh under cold running water. Add to the melted butter and toss to coat. Arrange on the grill rack, season and grill for 2–3 minutes on each side until golden.

❾ Place the soufflés in the middle of warmed serving plates and arrange the potato wedges around the edge with some watercress. Serve at once.

Teriyaki Salmon Parcels

SERVES 2

Cooking the fish inside paper ensures that all the flavours are intensified and the fish remains nice and moist.

1 large garlic clove
2.5cm (1in) piece of fresh root ginger
3 tablespoons sunflower oil
1 teaspoon clear honey
1 tablespoon dry sherry
4 tablespoons light soy sauce
2 salmon cutlets, each weighing about 100g (4oz)
100g (4oz) medium egg noodles
1 small red pepper
6 mange-tout peas
2 spring onions
50g (2oz) bean sprouts
1 teaspoon caster sugar
1 teaspoon sesame oil

1 Pre-heat the oven to 200°C/400°F/Gas 6.

2 Finely chop the garlic and ginger. Heat 1 tablespoon of the oil in a small frying pan, add half the garlic and half the ginger and fry for 1 minute until softened. Add the honey, sherry and half the soy sauce and allow to just bubble. Remove from the heat and leave to cool a little.

3 Carefully remove the centre bone from each salmon cutlet. Curl each cutlet around to form a medallion and tie with string.

Place each medallion in the centre of a 30.5cm (12in) square of parchment paper. Spoon the teriyaki sauce over each and draw up the corners of the paper. Seal to form parcels and place on a baking tray. Bake for 10 minutes until just cooked through.

4 Meanwhile, add the noodles to a saucepan of boiling water and cook for 4 minutes.

5 Cut the red pepper in half, remove the core and seeds then cut the flesh into diamonds. Cut the mange-tout diagonally into pieces. Slice the spring onions.

6 Heat a wok or large frying pan and add the remaining oil. Add the remaining garlic and ginger and cook for 10 seconds. Add the mange-tout and pepper and stir-fry for 1–2 minutes.

7 Drain the noodles and add to the wok with the spring onions, bean sprouts and sugar. Toss well until heated through. Sprinkle with the remaining soy sauce and the sesame oil and mix well together.

8 To serve, place the parcels on warmed serving plates, spoon the noodles around them and serve at once.

Hot and Sour Prawns in Seaweed Nests

SERVES 2

If you have never used fresh chillies before then take note. Once you have scooped out and discarded the seeds, scrub your hands. They are fiery and will tickle more than just your taste buds!

---

10 large tiger prawns, thawed if frozen

1 small red chilli

1 small garlic clove

juice of 1 lime

1 tablespoon light soy sauce

1 teaspoon sesame oil

1 tablespoon finely chopped fresh coriander

1 teaspoon lemon grass purée (optional)

15g (½oz) dried medium egg noodles

175g (6oz) spring greens

sunflower oil, for deep-frying

¼ teaspoon caster sugar

¼ teaspoon salt

25g (1oz) flaked almonds

2 chilli flowers, to garnish (see page 49)

❶ Pre-heat the grill. Peel the prawns, leaving the tails intact.

❷ Cut the chilli in half, and chop finely, discarding the seeds. Crush the garlic. Put both in a shallow non-metallic dish and add the lime juice, soy sauce, sesame oil, coriander and lemon grass, if using. Add the prawns and set aside.

❸ Cook the noodles in a saucepan of boiling salted water for 1 minute until just softened. Drain the noodles and refresh under cold water. Wrap a piece of noodle around each prawn, tucking in the ends, and arrange on a lightly oiled baking tray. Grill the prawns for 4–5 minutes until pink, turning once.

❹ Meanwhile, remove the thick stalks from the spring greens. Lay the leaves on top of each other, roll up tightly like a cigar, and carefully shred widthways into thin strands. Lightly run your fingers through them to separate the strands.

❺ Heat 2.5cm (1in) sunflower oil in a wok. Standing well back from the wok, add small handfuls of leaves. Fry for 30 seconds to 1 minute, remove with a slotted spoon and drain on kitchen paper, spreading the strands out so that the excess oil is absorbed. Sprinkle with the sugar and salt.

❻ Heat a frying pan. Add the almonds and dry-fry until toasted.

❼ To serve, put the 'seaweed' in Chinese bowls and scatter with the almonds. Arrange the prawns on top and garnish with the chilli flowers.

Seared Trout Fillets with Warm Salad Niçoise

SERVES 2

It's always best to buy your fish from a reputable fishmonger, and a smile and a wink will persuade him to fillet it for you.

1 small red chilli
2 trout fillets, with skin on
juice of ½ a lime
150g (5oz) small new potatoes
150g (5oz) cauliflower florets
75g (3oz) green beans
2 plum tomatoes
25g (1oz) hazelnuts
1 tablespoon lemon juice
3 tablespoons hazelnut oil
5 pitted black olives
salt and freshly ground black pepper
lime slices, to garnish

1 Chop the chilli, discarding the seeds and rub over the trout fillets with the lime juice. Leave to marinate.

2 Cut the potatoes in half. Put in a saucepan of cold salted water, cover, bring to the boil and cook for 10–15 minutes until tender.

3 Meanwhile, trim the cauliflower florets, tail the beans and cut in half. Roughly dice the tomatoes. Add the cauliflower and beans to the saucepan of potatoes and continue to cook until just tender. Add the tomatoes and return to the boil, then drain.

4 Put the hazelnuts in a frying pan and dry-fry until lightly toasted.

5 Roughly chop the hazelnuts and put into a bowl. Pour over the lemon juice, add the hazelnut oil, salt and pepper and whisk together.

6 Heat a griddle pan. Cook the trout on the griddle (a criss-cross marking on the skin will be made by cooking on it), season with salt and pepper and fry for 2 minutes on each side until cooked.

7 Drain the vegetables and, while still warm, pour over half of the dressing. Cut the olives in half and mix into the warm salad.

8 Serve the trout in the centre of warmed serving plates, surrounded by the warm salad. Pour the remaining hazelnut vinaigrette on top of the fish. Garnish with lime slices.

Mixed Seafood Pasta

SERVES 2

Making pasta dishes is a great way to learn to cook. You will often hear the term 'al dente'. This means to cook the pasta so that it has 'a bite'. In other words, don't overcook it.

175g (6oz) spaghetti
350g (12oz) fresh mussels
1 onion
120ml (4fl oz) white wine
1 bay leaf
1 celery stick
1 garlic clove
2 tablespoons olive oil
100g (4oz) thick cod fillet
200g (7oz) can chopped tomatoes
1 tablespoon tomato purée
½ teaspoon caster sugar
a small handful of fresh basil leaves, plus leaves to garnish
225g (8oz) mixed seafood cocktail
salt and freshly ground black pepper

1 Cook the spaghetti in a large saucepan of boiling water for 10 minutes until just tender.

2 Using a small, sharp knife, clean the unopened mussels under cold running water. Discard any mussels with cracked or open shells.

3 Trim the ends off the onion and put in a pan with the mussels, wine and bay leaf. Cover and cook over a high heat for 5 minutes until the mussel shells open shaking the pan occasionally.

4 Remove the onion from the pan. Chop the onion, dice the celery and crush the garlic. Heat the oil in a frying pan, add the onion, celery and garlic and cook for 3 minutes until beginning to soften.

5 Meanwhile, skin the cod fillet and cut into 2cm (¾in) chunks. Add the pieces of cod, tomatoes, tomato purée, sugar, salt and pepper to the pan and simmer for 2 minutes. Shred the handful of basil leaves, add to the pan with the mixed seafood and simmer for a further 3 minutes.

6 Using a slotted spoon, lift the mussels out of the pan. Discard any unopened mussels. Boil the cooking liquid rapidly until reduced by half. Strain the reduced cooking liquid into the seafood sauce.

7 Drain the spaghetti and toss in the seafood sauce.

8 Pile the seafood spaghetti on to warmed serving plates. Arrange the mussels around the edge and garnish with basil leaves.

Rosti-Crusted Sole with Tarragon Sauce

SERVES 2

When making rosti potatoes, it's important to use 'waxy' potatoes. After grating they need to be rinsed in a sieve and dried really well.

1 shallot
1 small leek
75g (3oz) unsalted butter, plus extra for greasing
1 waxy potato, weighing about 175g (6oz)
four 75g (3oz) lemon sole fillets, skinned
1 egg yolk
about 150ml (¼ pint) dry white wine
1 small fennel head
1 tablespoon sunflower oil
75g (3oz) French beans
grated rind and juice of 1 lemon
150ml (¼ pint) fish stock (from a carton)
50g (2oz) mange-tout peas
75ml (3fl oz) double cream
a small bunch of fresh tarragon
salt and freshly ground black pepper

❶ Pre-heat the oven to 200°C/400°F/Gas 6.
❷ Finely chop the shallot and leek. Melt 25g (1oz) of the butter in a saucepan. Add the shallot and leek and cook for 6–8 minutes over a low heat until well softened.

❸ Coarsely grate the potato in a food processor or on a box grater. Put in a sieve and rinse well. Dry on kitchen paper. Heat a frying pan. Add 25g (1oz) of the butter to the pan, add the potato and cook for 2–3 minutes, stirring. Remove from the heat and transfer to a bowl.

❹ Fold the fish fillets in half, with the skinned side inwards, and arrange on a buttered baking tray. Mix the egg yolk into the potato and season well with salt and pepper. Divide the potato mixture between the top of the fillets. Place in the oven for 8–10 minutes until the fish is tender and the rosti is crisp.

❺ Meanwhile, add the wine to the shallot and leek, bring to the boil and reduce to one-third.

❻ Thinly slice the fennel. Heat the oil and remaining butter in a wok or large frying pan. Add the fennel and beans and stir-fry for 1 minute. Add 3 tablespoons of water or wine and the lemon juice and steam-fry for 2–3 minutes.

❼ Pour the fish stock into the wine mixture and reduce by half. Add the mange-tout and lemon rind and stir-fry for a further 1–2 minutes until all the liquid has evaporated. Season with salt and pepper. Add the cream and bring to a simmer. Chop the tarragon, add to the sauce and remove from the heat.

8 Arrange the soles on warmed serving plates. Spoon some of the sauce around them, add some of the vegetables and serve at once.

Salmon and Prawn Puff Pie

SERVES 2

Cooking has never been easier. Not only can you buy ready-made puff pastry, but also ready-made, ready-rolled puff pastry. So, come on, you have no excuse for not trying this lovely little dish.

175g (6oz) ready-made ready-rolled puff pastry
beaten egg, to glaze
1 small fennel head
2 tablespoons olive oil
10 thin asparagus tips
1 shallot
1 tablespoon sunflower oil
150ml (¼ pint) dry white wine
175g (6oz) salmon fillet, skinned
a little lemon juice
15g (½oz) butter, softened
1 teaspoon plain flour
3 tablespoons crème fraiche
100g (4oz) peeled cooked prawns
salt and freshly ground black pepper

1 Pre-heat the oven to 200°C/400°F/Gas 6.

2 Place the pastry on a floured surface and cut out two 12.5cm (5in) rounds. Place on a baking tray, score with a knife, brush with egg and bake for 10 minutes until well risen and golden.

3 Remove any feathery leaves from the fennel and reserve. Finely slice the fennel. Heat a griddle pan or heavy frying pan. Mix together the olive oil, salt and pepper and dip the fennel in the oil then put the slices on the griddle. Coat the asparagus in a little of the oil and add to the griddle. Cook the vegetables until slightly charred, turning once, then put on a warmed plate.

4 Finely chop the shallot. Heat the sunflower oil in a saucepan and fry the shallot gently for 1 minute. Add the wine and boil rapidly to reduce by half to a syrup.

5 Slice the salmon into 4 long thin strips. Season with salt and pepper and add to the griddle the vegetables were cooked on. Cook for 1 minute then turn the strips and squeeze a little lemon juice over them. Turn off the heat and let the salmon cook on the warmth of the pan.

6 Blend together the butter and flour until smooth then whisk into the wine mixture, a little at a time. Add the crème fraiche and stir until thickened. Stir in the prawns. Chop and add the reserved fennel leaves.

❼ To serve, slice the cooked pastry puffs horizontally through the middle and place the bottoms on 2 warmed serving plates.

Spoon the prawn mixture over them and arrange the salmon strips on top. Cover with the pastry lids, letting the salmon peep out of the edges. Fan the fennel to one side and arrange the asparagus on top.

Cod and Crab Gratin

SERVES 2

This recipe, once you have tried and tasted the result, lends itself perfectly to being 'tampered' with. Try adding some finely shredded lemon grass, a little fresh ginger, in fact anything that takes your fancy.

225g (8oz) waxy new potatoes
175ml (6fl oz) milk
a few black peppercorns
1 bay leaf
275g (10oz) cod fillet, skinned
100g (4oz) button mushrooms
40g (1½oz) butter
1 tablespoon plain flour
100g (4oz) white crab meat
1 teaspoon Dijon mustard
1 tablespoon chopped fresh parsley
50g (2oz) Cheddar cheese
150g (5oz) small broccoli florets
salt and freshly ground black pepper

❶ Without peeling, thickly slice the potatoes and put in a saucepan of cold salted water. Bring to the boil and cook for about 10 minutes until just tender.

❷ Meanwhile, put the milk, peppercorns and bay leaf in a small saucepan and bring to a simmer. Cut the cod into 2.5cm (1in) pieces, add to the pan and poach for 2–3 minutes until just tender.

❸ Slice the mushrooms. Melt half the butter in a small pan, add the mushrooms and stir to coat. Cook for 2–3 minutes until golden.

❹ Place the cod in the bottom of an ovenproof dish, cover with foil and keep warm. Strain the milk and reserve. Discard the bay leaf and peppercorns.

❺ Stir the flour into the mushroom mixture and cook for 1 minute. Remove from the heat and gradually stir in the reserved milk until smooth. Slowly bring to the boil, stirring constantly, and cook for 2–3 minutes until thickened and smooth. Stir in the crab meat, mustard, parsley and season with salt and pepper to taste. Heat through gently. Pour over the cod and level with a palette knife.

❻ Pre-heat the grill. Drain the potatoes and refresh under cold running water. Leave to cool slightly then arrange the potatoes over the crab mixture. Grate the cheese and sprinkle on top. Grill for 2–3 minutes until bubbling.

7 Heat the remaining butter and 2 tablespoons of water in a wok or frying pan. Add the broccoli and steam-fry for 2–3 minutes until just tender. Serve at once with the gratin.

Seafood Chowder

SERVES 2

Serving the chowder in bread rolls not only provides a nutritional filler but also looks authentically rustic.

2 large crisp rustic bread rolls, at least 15cm (6in) in diameter
1 tablespoon sunflower oil
a knob of unsalted butter
50g (2oz) diced smoked bacon
1 small onion
1 small celery stick
1 small carrot
75g (3oz) potato
1 heaped tablespoon plain flour
150ml (¼ pint) fish or vegetable stock
300ml (½ pint) milk
1 bay leaf
150g (5oz) uncoloured cod, skinned
a small bunch of fresh chives
50g (2oz) peeled cooked prawns
120ml (4fl oz) single cream
a pinch of cayenne
salt and freshly ground black pepper

1 Pre-heat the oven to 200°C/400°F/Gas 6.

2 Cut the tops off each roll, scoop out and discard the centres and place on a baking tray. Bake for 8–10 minutes until crisp.

3 Heat the oil and butter in a frying pan and fry the bacon for 4–5 minutes until crispy. Chop the onion and celery. Peel and chop the carrot. Peel and dice the potato. Add the vegetables to the pan and cook for 5 minutes until the onion is softened.

4 Stir in the flour and cook for 1 minute, then gradually pour in the stock and milk, stirring all the time until smooth. Add the bay leaf and bring to the boil, stirring.

5 Cut the cod into small bite-sized pieces and add to the pan. Simmer for about 5 minutes until the fish and potatoes are tender.

6 Snip the chives, reserving 6 whole ones. Stir the snipped chives into the soup with the prawns and cook to just warm through. Stir in the cream. Season with salt and pepper to taste.

7 When cooked, remove the bread rolls from the oven and place each one in a soup bowl. Ladle the soup into the bread rolls and garnish with the reserved chives. Sprinkle with a little cayenne and serve at once.

Chinese Pancake Rolls

SERVES 2

This all-time favourite Chinese dish is certain to impress whoever you are serving it to. It becomes even nicer when accompanied by a lightly dressed salad.

50g (2oz) plain flour
25g (1oz) cornflour
2 eggs
about 6 tablespoons sunflower oil
2.5cm (1in) piece of fresh root ginger
2 garlic cloves
4 spring onions, plus 2 spring onion tassels (see below)
50g (2oz) cooked ham
1 small carrot
100g (4oz) peeled cooked prawns
7 tablespoons dark soy sauce
2 teaspoons sugar
50g (2oz) fresh bean sprouts
1 small red chilli
salt and freshly ground black pepper

- - -

Spring onion tassels *To make spring onion tassels, cut the onions into 5cm (2in) lengths, discarding the roots and tops. Using a sharp knife, make as many fine cuts as possible down the onions, taking care not to cut all the way to the bottom so the tassel will hold together. Put into a bowl of iced water for at least 20 minutes to open out.*

1 Sift the flour, cornflour and a pinch of salt into a bowl. In a jug, beat the eggs, 1 tablespoon of the oil and 120ml (4fl oz) water until smooth. Make a well in the centre of the flour mixture and gradually pour in the liquid, stirring, to make a smooth, fairly thin, batter. Leave to stand for 5 minutes.

2 Peel and finely chop the ginger. Finely chop the garlic, spring onions and ham. Peel and coarsely grate the carrot. Heat 1 tablespoon of the oil in a frying pan. Add half the ginger and the garlic and stir-fry for 1 minute. Add the spring onions, carrot, ham, prawns, 1 tablespoon of the soy sauce and half the sugar and stir-fry for 1–2 minutes. Season with salt and pepper to taste.

3 Add the bean sprouts and cook for a further 1–2 minutes, then tip into a sieve to drain off any excess moisture. Leave to cool completely.

4 Heat a large heavy-based frying pan and brush with a little of the oil. Pour in about a quarter of the batter so that it thinly coats the pan.

5 Cook the pancake until the edges begin to curl and the top is cooked through. Do not turn it over. Transfer to a warmed plate and repeat to make 3 more pancakes, leaving a little batter for sealing.

6 Divide the filling into quarters and place one portion down one edge of the top side of a pancake. Roll up the pancake to enclose the filling, folding in the edges and sealing with a little of the remaining batter as you go. Repeat to make 4 spring rolls.

7 Heat about 4 tablespoons of oil in the frying pan and fry the pancake rolls for about 5 minutes, turning occasionally until lightly golden all over.

8 Meanwhile, cut the chilli in half, remove the seeds and finely chop the flesh. Mix together the remaining 6 tablespoons of soy sauce, remaining ginger, remaining sugar and the chilli.

9 Drain the spring rolls on kitchen paper and arrange 2 on each warmed serving plate. Garnish with the spring onion tassels and serve hot with the chilli dipping sauce.

DESSERTS

Sticky Toffee Pudding

SERVES 4

If you don't like or are allergic to nuts, simply leave them out. If, however, you are using them, be sure to toast them really well to bring out the full flavour in the dish.

75g (3oz) unsalted butter
100g (4oz) plus 1 tablespoon light muscovado sugar
6 tablespoons golden syrup
275g (10oz) shop-bought chocolate slab cake
1 tablespoon brandy
50g (2oz) walnut pieces
a few drops of vanilla essence
150ml (¼ pint) double cream
1 large orange
1 small mango
1 large banana
vanilla ice cream, to serve
icing sugar, to dust
mint sprigs, to decorate

1 Pre-heat the oven to 200°C/400°F/Gas 6.

2 Put 50g (2oz) of the butter, the 100g (4oz) muscovado sugar and the golden syrup in a saucepan and heat gently until the sugar dissolves.

3 Meanwhile, cut the cake into thick, even slices and arrange in a small, buttered roasting tin. Sprinkle with the brandy.

4 Increase the heat of the sugar mixture and cook for 3–4 minutes until thickened and syrupy.

5 Put the walnuts in a small frying pan and dry-fry until toasted. Sprinkle the walnuts over the chocolate slices.

6 Add the vanilla essence and cream to the sugar mixture and cook for a further 1–2 minutes, stirring. Pour the toffee sauce over the cake to coat it completely. Place in the oven and bake for 10–12 minutes until the sauce is bubbling and the cake is lightly toasted.

7 Meanwhile, pare the rind from the orange and squeeze out the juice. Peel the mango, slice the flesh as close as possible down either side of the central stone, then cut away the flesh. Slice into bite-sized pieces. Melt the remaining butter in a frying pan. Peel and thickly slice the banana. Add to the pan with the mango and sprinkle with the remaining tablespoon of sugar. Fry for 2–3 minutes until just beginning to soften. Pour in the orange juice, add the rind and bring to the boil.

8 Pre-heat the grill. Flash the pudding under the grill to lightly toast and spoon on to warmed serving plates. Add the fruit mixture and a scoop of the ice-cream. Dust with icing sugar, decorate with mint sprigs and serve at once.

Apple Tarts

SERVES 2

Kitchen gadgets can save you a lot of time and trouble – none more so than an apple wedger.

1 small Cox's apple

25g (1oz) butter

two 7.5cm (3in) dessert pastry tartlets

2 heaped tablespoons apricot conserve

icing sugar, to dust

mint sprigs, to decorate

pouring cream, to serve

1 Pre-heat the oven to 200°C/400°F/Gas 6.

2 Using an apple wedger, cut the apple into wedges. Heat the butter in a small frying pan. Add the apple wedges and toss to coat. Cook for 1–2 minutes.

3 Place the tartlets on a baking tray and spoon a little of the apricot conserve into the bottom of each. Arrange the apples on top. Spoon over the remaining apricot conserve.

4 Bake in the oven for 8–10 minutes until bubbling.

5 Place on serving plates and dust with icing sugar. Decorate with mint sprigs and drizzle over a little cream. Serve at once.

Chocolate Truffle Cake

SERVES 8–12

The use of white and dark chocolate gives a stunning appearance to the finished look of this cake. It's very important to use good quality plain chocolate, so choose one with at least 70 per cent cocoa solids.

2 eggs

50g (2oz) caster sugar

125g (5oz) white chocolate

50g (2oz) plain flour

2 tablespoons golden syrup

150ml (¼ pint) double cream

150g (5oz) plain chocolate

2 tablespoons rum

cocoa powder or icing sugar, to dust

1 Pre-heat the oven to 190°C/375°F/Gas 5. Grease and line a 23cm (9in) round cake tin.

2 Put the eggs and sugar into a large heatproof bowl and set over a saucepan of simmering water. Whisk until thick enough to leave a trail when the whisk is raised. Remove from the heat.

3 Finely grate 25g (1oz) of the white

chocolate. Using a metal spoon, carefully fold the chocolate and flour into the egg mixture. Turn into the prepared tin and bake for 12–15 minutes, until firm to the touch.

4 Meanwhile, break the remaining white chocolate into a large heatproof bowl, stand over the pan of simmering water and heat until melted. Stir in the syrup and beat with a wooden spoon to make a paste. Remove from the heat. Cover with clingfilm and leave for 5 minutes.

5 Pour the cream into a small pan, break in the plain chocolate and heat gently, stirring until melted. Transfer to a clean bowl and whisk until thick.

6 Remove the cooked cake from the oven and turn out of the tin on to a wire cooling rack. Drizzle over the rum. Spread the chocolate truffle mixture over the sponge, spreading a little down the sides.

7 Roll the icing into 3 balls then roll out thinly into 10cm (4in) circles. Cut the circles in half and crimp the curved edges with your fingers to make them wavy. Press them around the top edge of the cake. Dust with icing sugar or cocoa powder before serving.

Lemon Creams

SERVES 2

This is the pudding which will really impress your friends and family – rich, creamy, zesty and easy to make.

300ml (½ pint) double cream
75g (3oz) caster sugar
grated rind and juice of 1 lemon
150ml (¼ pint) double cream
4 strawberries
icing sugar, to dust
sweet biscuits, to serve

1 Put the cream and sugar in a saucepan and bring to the boil, stirring until the sugar dissolves. Add the lemon juice and stir until thickened. Remove from the heat and allow to cool a little.

2 Pour into glass serving dishes and leave to set in the fridge.

3 Whip the cream until it just holds its shape. Spoon the whipped cream into a piping bag fitted with a large star nozzle and pipe rosettes on to the top of the lemon creams.

3 Slice the strawberries and arrange on top of the cream. Scatter with the lemon rind and dust with icing sugar. Serve with sweet biscuits.

Poached Pears in Red Wine

SERVES 2

The sponge biscuits can be made a few days before required, providing they are stored in an airtight container. If you don't feel confident about feathering the cream practise well in advance.

100g (4oz) caster sugar
300ml (½ pint) red wine
1 cinnamon stick
4 ripe pears
about 1 teaspoon arrowroot
150ml (¼ pint) double cream
150g (5oz) carton Greek strained yogurt
icing sugar, to dust
FOR THE SPONGE BISCUITS
50g (2oz) unsalted butter
50g (2oz) caster sugar
a few drops of vanilla essence
a pinch of freshly grated nutmeg
1 large egg white
50g (2oz) plain flour

❶ Pre-heat the oven to 200°C/400°F/Gas 6. Put the sugar and wine in a saucepan. Break the cinnamon stick in half, add to the pan and bring slowly to the boil, stirring until the sugar has dissolved.

❷ Meanwhile, peel the pears then remove the cores through the base, keeping the pears intact. Add the pears to the pan, cover with a round of greaseproof paper and then a lid and poach gently for 10 minutes or until just tender, turning occasionally.

❸ To make the sponge biscuits, cream together the butter and sugar until soft and fluffy. Add the vanilla essence and nutmeg. Whisk the egg white in a large bowl until it just holds its shape. Gradually beat the egg white into the creamed mixture then fold in the flour.

❹ Drop teaspoons of the mixture on to a baking tray lined with parchment paper, allowing space for the biscuits to spread. Bake for 6–8 minutes until set and lightly golden around the edges.

❺ Using a slotted spoon, remove the pears from the cooking liquid and place on a plate. Discard the cinnamon. Boil the remaining liquid until reduced by half. Blend the arrowroot with a little water, add to the syrup and stir until thickened.

❻ Reserve 2 teaspoons of cream for decoration and whip the remaining cream until it just holds its shape. Fold in the yogurt.

❼ Remove the cooked biscuits from the oven and leave to cool on a wire rack.

❽ To serve, place 2 pears on each serving plate and spoon around some of the syrup. Using a cocktail stick, feather the cream into the syrup. Layer the biscuits with the cream and yogurt mixture and arrange on the plates. Dust with icing sugar and serve at once.

Queen of Puddings with Banana Custard

SERVES 2

The banana custard really lifts the flavour of this great old English pudding.

300ml (½ pint) milk
150ml (¼ pint) double cream
½ teaspoon vanilla essence
1 small lemon
100g (4oz) fresh white breadcrumbs
25g (1oz) unsalted butter
75g (3oz) caster sugar
4–6 tablespoons raspberry jam
2 eggs
150g (5oz) carton natural yogurt
2 teaspoons clear honey
2 small bananas

❶ Put the milk, cream and vanilla essence in a saucepan and bring to the boil. Grate in the lemon rind then stir in the breadcrumbs, butter and 25g (1oz) of the sugar. Cook over a low heat for 2–3 minutes, stirring. Pour into a 900ml (1½ pint) ovenproof dish and leave for about 5 minutes to allow a skin to form.

❷ Pre-heat the oven to 220°C/450°F/ Gas 8.

❸ Put the jam in a small pan over a low heat, until melted.

❹ Separate the eggs. Whisk the egg whites in a large bowl until stiff, then quickly whisk in the remaining sugar. Spoon into a piping bag fitted with a large star nozzle.

❺ Sieve the jam over the surface of the pudding, then pipe the meringue mixture on top. Place in the oven and bake for about 5 minutes until the meringue is golden.

❻ Meanwhile, make the custard. Put the egg yolks in a small pan with the yogurt and honey and place over a low heat. Cut the bananas into thin slices and add to the pan. Cook until the mixture boils and thickens, stirring constantly.

❼ Serve the pudding hot, with plenty of custard.

Toffee Fruit with Instant Lychee Ice Cream

SERVES 4

Deep-fried fruit makes a great pudding for Sunday lunch. Be careful when putting the fruit into the hot fat and don't overfill the pan with oil. It's crucial that the lychees are frozen to make the ice cream.

40g (1½oz) plain flour

2 tablespoons cornflour

1 teaspoon baking powder

2 teaspoons sesame oil

groundnut oil, for frying

2 small bananas

1 large eating apple

175g (6oz) caster sugar

2 tablespoons sesame seeds

400g (14oz) can lychees in syrup, drained and frozen until solid

150ml (¼ pint) double cream

---

❶ Sift the flour, cornflour and baking powder into a bowl. Mix together 75ml (3fl oz) water and half the sesame oil. Make a well in the centre of the flour mixture and gradually pour in the liquid, stirring until smooth. Set aside.

❷ Heat about 4cm (1½in) of the groundnut oil and the remaining sesame oil in a wok.

❸ Peel the bananas, then split them in half lengthways and cut into 4cm (1½in) chunks. Peel the apple then, using an apple wedger, cut into wedges. Stir the fruit pieces into the batter mixture then, using a slotted spoon, remove and drain off the excess batter.

❹ Deep-fry the fruit for about 2–3 minutes until golden. Remove with a slotted spoon and drain on kitchen paper. Repeat until all the fruit has been cooked.

❺ Meanwhile, put the sugar, sesame seeds and 2 tablespoons of groundnut oil in a small pan. Heat for about 5 minutes brushing down the sides occasionally with a pastry brush dipped in water, until light brown and caramelised.

❻ When the caramel is made, add a few pieces of the fruit and stir gently to coat. Then quickly take them out and plunge into a bowl of ice-cold water for a few seconds to make the caramel harden.

❼ Put the frozen lychees and cream in a food processor and whiz until blended into an instant ice cream.

❽ Remove the toffee fruit from the water and serve at once with a scoop of the ice cream.

Baskets of Chocolate Praline with Mango Sauce

SERVES 2

Praline is simply a combination of nuts and caramel which has been crushed. It can be made in advance and stored in an airtight container for use as and when required.

50g (2oz) sugar
50g (2oz) chopped mixed nuts
2 brandy snaps
1 ripe mango
juice of ½ a lime
2 tablespoons chocolate hazelnut spread
100g (4oz) mascarpone cheese
1 tablespoon double cream
mint springs, to decorate
a little icing sugar, to dust

1 Pre-heat the oven to 180°C/350°F/Gas 4.

2 To make the praline, put the sugar and 2 tablespoons of water into a heavy-based saucepan and stir over a high heat until dissolved completely. Boil rapidly until light golden brown, then stir in the nuts and continue to cook until golden brown.

3 Meanwhile, place the brandy snaps on a baking tray and put into the oven for about 30 seconds until uncurled.

4 When the caramel is golden brown, tip on to a baking tray lined with parchment paper. Spread as flat as you can and leave to harden.

5 Remove the brandy snaps from the oven and, using a fish-slice carefully lift off the baking tray and shape over small dariole moulds to make baskets. Leave to cool.

6 Cut the cheeks from the mango, as close as possible down either side of the stone. Cut a criss-cross of lines through the flesh, not allowing the knife to pierce the skin. Fold inside out to create a hedgehog effect.

7 Cut the cubes and put into a food processor. Add the lime juice and blend to form a purée. Sieve the purée to remove any stringy pieces.

8 Mix together the chocolate spread and mascarpone cheese. Using a rolling pin or a mortar and pestle, crush half of the praline into a powder. Stir 2 tablespoons of the praline into the chocolate mixture. Fill a piping bag, fitted with a large star nozzle, with the chocolate mixture and pipe the cream into the brandy snap baskets.

9 To serve, flood the serving plates with the mango sauce. Dot the sauce with 3 spots of cream and, using a cocktail stick, feather the cream into the mango sauce. Place the baskets on top. Break off a couple of pieces of the remaining praline and place in the chocolate praline. Decorate with mint sprigs and a dusting of icing sugar.

Dariole moulds *are small, narrow moulds with sloping sides and are used for making rum babas, madeleines and individual desserts. If you don't have any you could use small heatproof glasses or teacups.*

Crêpes Suzette

SERVES 2

The art of making good pancakes is to use as little batter as you dare and wiggle the pan around so that the mixture spreads evenly.

75g (3oz) plain flour
a pinch of salt
1 egg
150ml (¼ pint) milk
1 miniature bottle of Grand Marnier or Cointreau (about 3 tablespoons)
sunflower oil, for frying
50g (2oz) unsalted butter
50g (2oz) caster sugar
1 large orange, plus 2 orange slices to decorate
icing sugar, to dust
mint sprigs, to decorate

❶ Sift the flour and salt into a bowl and make a well in the centre. Beat together the egg and milk then gradually beat into the flour, drawing in the flour from the sides, to make a smooth batter. Stir in a small splash of the liqueur.

❷ Heat a large heavy-based frying pan with a little oil. Ladle in just enough batter to thinly coat the base of the pan and cook for about 1 minute until golden.

❸ Turn or toss over the crêpe and cook for about another 30 seconds. Repeat with the remaining batter to make 4 pancakes. Layer the pancakes between sheets of parchment paper.

❹ In another large frying pan, heat the butter and sugar until thick and syrupy.

❺ Meanwhile, finely grate the rind from the large orange and squeeze out the juice. Add to the pan with another splash of the liqueur.

❻ Meanwhile, fold the crêpes into triangles by folding each one in half and then in half again. Place them in the frying pan with the sauce and spoon the sauce over the crêpes to coat them evenly.

❼ In a ladle or small pan, gently heat the remaining liqueur. Pour over the crêpes and set alight, basting until the flames die down.

❽ Make a cut into the centre of the orange slices then twist in opposite directions. Serve the crêpes with a dusting of icing sugar and decorated with mint sprigs and the orange twists.

Expresso Soufflés

SERVES 4

If you want to make this into a real 'dinner party dish' cook and serve the soufflés in small expresso coffee cups for an attractive presentation.

15g (½oz) unsalted butter
50g (2oz) caster sugar, plus extra to dust
150g (5oz) plain chocolate
4 tablespoons strong instant coffee
2 eggs
1 teaspoon plain flour
75ml (3fl oz) double cream
1 tablespoon brandy
8 strawberry fans, to decorate (see below)
icing sugar and cocoa powder, to dust
vanilla ice cream, to serve

❶ Pre-heat the oven to 220°C/425°F/ Gas 7. Butter four 100ml (4fl oz) ramekin dishes and dust with a little caster sugar.

❷ Break 75g (3oz) of the chocolate into a heatproof bowl and stand it over a saucepan of simmering water. Add half of the coffee and heat, stirring occasionally, until the chocolate has melted. Remove from the heat and leave to cool a little.

❸ Separate the eggs. Whisk the whites in a large bowl until stiff, then whisk in half the sugar until stiff and glossy.

❹ Stir the egg yolks, flour and the remaining sugar into the chocolate mixture.

❺ Fold a quarter of the egg whites into the chocolate mixture, then carefully fold in the remaining egg whites.

❻ Divide the mixture equally between the prepared dishes and place on a baking tray. Bake for 10–12 minutes until well risen.

❼ Meanwhile, break the remaining chocolate into a small heavy-based saucepan. Add the remaining coffee, the cream and brandy and stir over a low heat for a few minutes until shiny and smooth.

❽ Arrange the strawberry fans around the serving plates to decorate, then dust with icing sugar and cocoa powder. Place a soufflé in the centre and cut a split in the middle. Add a scoop of ice cream and pour in some of the sauce. Serve at once.

Strawberry fans *To make strawberry fans, make 4–8 cuts (depending on their size) in the strawberries, taking care not to slice all the way through, then press gently so that the slices fan out.*

Autumn Crumble with Orange and Grand Marnier Custard

SERVES 2

The important thing about using the rind from oranges or lemons is to ensure that all the pith has been removed. If not, the result can be very bitter.

3 plums
1 large Bramley apple
25g (1oz) unsalted butter
1 firm pear
2 tablespoons sugar
a pinch of ground cloves
1 orange
3–4 tablespoons Grand Marnier
50g (2oz) pecan nuts
200g (7oz) packet of shortbread fingers
150ml (¼ pint) milk
150ml (¼ pint) double cream
4 egg yolks
40g (1½oz) caster sugar

❶ Pre-heat the oven to 200°C/400°F/Gas 6.

❷ Stone and slice the plums. Peel, core and chop the apple. Heat a frying pan, add the butter, apple and plums and fry gently. Peel, core and slice the pear and add to the pan with the sugar and cloves. Using a vegetable peeler, pare the rind from the orange. Put 2 strips in with the fruit to flavour and keep the rest for the custard. Add 2 tablespoons of Grand Marnier to the pan and cook until most of the liquid has evaporated.

❸ Meanwhile, heat a small frying pan and dry-fry the nuts, shaking the pan, until toasted.

❹ Put the nuts and shortbread into a food processor and blend to form crumbs.

❺ Tip the fruit into an ovenproof dish, removing the orange rind. Top with the crumble then bake in the oven for 8–10 minutes until golden brown.

❻ Meanwhile, heat the milk, cream and reserved orange rind in a saucepan. Whisk the egg yolks and sugar together. Pour the hot milk on to the eggs, whisking continuously, then strain the liquid back into the pan, discarding the orange rind. Add the remaining Grand Marnier and stir over a gentle heat until thick enough to coat the back of a wooden spoon.

❼ Pour the custard into a jug and serve with the crumble.

Pan-Fried Bread and Butter Puddings

SERVES 2

This is a great pudding for children to cook, and the earlier they start cooking the less likely they are to grow up to be reluctant cooks.

8 medium-thick slices of white bread
100g (4oz) butter
4 tablespoons dried mixed fruit
40g (1½oz) caster sugar
½ teaspoon ground cinnamon
2 tablespoons sunflower oil
1 large egg
150ml (¼ pint) double cream
¼ teaspoon vanilla essence
100g (4oz) milk chocolate
25g (1oz) light muscovado sugar
200ml (7fl oz) crème fraiche
cocoa powder and icing sugar, to dust
tiny mint sprigs, to decorate

❶ Using an 8.5cm (3½in) round fluted cutter, cut out a round from each slice of bread. Spread each slice with some of the butter.

❷ Divide 2 tablespoons of the dried fruit among 4 of the rounds, leaving a 5mm (¼in) border around the edges. Place the remaining rounds on top, butter-side down, and gently press the edges together to seal.

❸ Mix together the caster sugar and cinnamon and spread out on a plate.

❹ Heat 25g (1oz) of the remaining butter and the oil in a frying pan. Beat the egg in a bowl with 3 tablespoons of the cream and the vanilla essence. Dip the bread rounds into the egg mixture, one at a time, until well soaked and completely coated. Place them all on a plate. When the butter and oil are sizzling, arrange the rounds in the pan and cook over a moderate heat for 2 minutes on each side until golden.

❺ Break the chocolate into a small, heavy-based saucepan. Add the remaining 50g (2oz) of butter, the remaining cream and the muscovado sugar and blend over a low heat until smooth and shiny, stirring continuously.

❻ Using a fish slice, remove the rounds from the pan and quickly drain on kitchen paper. Using tongs, toss the rounds in the cinnamon sugar.

❼ Arrange the bread and butter puddings on warmed serving plates and drizzle over some of the sauce. Using 2 dessertspoons, shape the crème fraiche into egg shapes and place on the plates. Dust the plates liberally with cocoa powder and icing sugar and decorate with the mint sprigs. Add the remaining 2 tablespoons of dried fruit, heaped in 3 mounds around each plate, and top with mint sprigs. Serve at once.

Floating Islands and Apricot Custard

SERVES 2

Meringue is simple to make providing the bowl and whisk are clean and grease-free and the sugar is folded carefully into the egg whites.

2 large eggs
225g (9oz) caster sugar
a good pinch of ground cinnamon
1 teaspoon white wine vinegar
1 heaped teaspoon cornflour
175ml (6fl oz) milk
1 tablespoon flaked almonds
400g (14oz) can apricot halves in natural juice, drained
mint sprigs, to decorate
icing sugar, to dust

❶ Pre-heat the oven to 180°C/350°F/Gas 4.

❷ Separate the eggs. Put the egg whites in a large bowl and whisk until stiff and holding their shape. Whisk in 50g (2oz) of the sugar then fold in another 50g (2oz) of the sugar with the cinnamon, vinegar and cornflour.

❸ Using 2 large serving spoons, shape the meringue into 6 egg shapes, and arrange, spaced well apart, on a large baking tray lined with baking parchment. Bake for about 10 minutes until lightly browned but still soft in the middle.

❹ Meanwhile, pour the milk into a small saucepan and bring to a simmer. Put the egg yolks and 25g (1oz) of the sugar in a food processor and whiz for 2 minutes. Pour the warmed milk through the feeder tube and whiz for a further 2–3 seconds. Pour into a bowl, stand it over a saucepan of simmering water, and cook for about 10 minutes until thickened, stirring occasionally.

❺ Put the almonds in a small frying pan and dry-fry, shaking the pan, until toasted.

❻ Put the remaining 100g (4oz) sugar and 2 tablespoons of water in a small pan and heat until dissolved, brushing down the sides of the pan with a pastry brush dipped in water. Increase the heat and boil rapidly until the caramel is golden brown, without stirring but brushing down the sides of the pan occasionally.

❼ Reserving 2 of the apricot halves, roughly chop the apricots and place in a sieve standing over a bowl. With the back of a wooden spoon, push the apricots through the sieve to form a purée. Stir into the custard and heat gently until warm.

❽ Flood the serving plates with the custard and arrange 3 meringues on each plate. Slice the reserved apricots and scatter on top. Drizzle over the caramel in a lacy web and decorate with the almonds and mint sprigs. Dust with icing sugar and serve at once.

Tarte Tatin with Praline Cream

SERVES 4

This is an upside-down tart, so much simpler to produce than a conventional one. Once you have tried this recipe, experiment with other ingredients of a similar texture to apples, such as mangoes and pears.

25g (1oz) butter

25g (1oz) light muscovado sugar

5 small eating apples, such as Cox's

100g (4oz) puff pastry, thawed if frozen

50g (2oz) caster sugar

sunflower oil, for brushing

15g (½oz) flaked almonds

75g (3oz) full-fat soft cream cheese

50g (2oz) crème fraiche

mint sprigs, to decorate

1 Pre-heat the oven to 220°C/425°F/Gas 7.

2 Heat the butter and muscovado sugar in a 20cm (8in) ovenproof frying pan, until the butter has melted, the sugar dissolved and the mixture is golden.

3 Meanwhile, peel the apples, cut into quarters and remove the cores. Add to the pan, turn to coat and cook until they start to caramelise.

4 Meanwhile, on a lightly floured surface roll out the pastry into a round a little larger than the pan.

5 Place the pastry round over the apples, tucking in the edges until it fits the pan neatly. Prick lightly with a fork. Bake in the oven for about 10–15 minutes until the pastry is risen and golden.

6 Put 40g (1½oz) of the caster sugar and 2 tablespoons of water in a saucepan and heat gently until dissolved, brushing the sides with a pastry brush dipped in water. Continue cooking the sugar syrup, without stirring, for about 10 minutes until golden.

7 Line a baking tray with foil and brush lightly with oil. Chop the flaked almonds into small pieces. Pour the syrup in a very thin, even layer over the lined baking tray then quickly sprinkle with the nuts. Leave to set.

8 Meanwhile, beat the remaining caster sugar into the cream cheese until the sugar has dissolved. Fold in the crème fraiche.

9 Break the praline into small pieces. Reserving half for decoration, fold the rest into the cream. Remove the cooked tart from the oven, place a large plate on top of the pan and invert the tart on to it. Decorate with the remaining praline pieces and serve with spoonfuls of the praline cream, topped with mint sprigs.

Index